WESLEYAN POETRY

Also by CALVIN C. HERNTON

POETRY

The Coming of Chronos to the House of Nightsong:
An Epical Narrative of the South (1964)

Medicine Man: Collected Poems (1976)

The Red Crab Gang and Black River Poems (1999)

FICTION

Scarecrow, novel (1974)

NONFICTION

Sex and Racism in America (1965)

White Papers for White Americans (1966)

Coming Together: Black Power, White Hatred, and
Sexual Hang-ups (1971)

The Cannabis Experience: An Interpretative Study
of the Effects of Marijuana and Hashish
(with Joseph Berke, 1974)

The Sexual Mountain and Black Women Writers:
Adventures in Sex, Literature, and Real Life (1987)

PLAYS

Glad to Be Dead (1958)

Flame (1958)

The Place (1972)

Selected Poems of
Calvin C. Hernton

Selected Poems of
Calvin C. Hernton

Edited by DAVID GRUNDY *and* LAURI SCHEYER

Foreword by ISHMAEL REED

WESLEYAN UNIVERSITY PRESS ✳ MIDDLETOWN, CONNECTICUT

Wesleyan University Press
Middletown CT 06459
www.wesleyan.edu/wespress

Manufactured in the United States of America
Designed and composed in Arno Pro by Eric M. Brooks

Library of Congress Cataloging-in-Publication Data
NAMES: Hernton, Calvin C., author. | Grundy, David, editor. |
    Scheyer, Lauri, editor. | Reed, Ishmael, 1938– writer of foreword.
TITLE: Selected poems of Calvin C. Hernton / edited by David Grundy
    and Lauri Scheyer; foreword by Ishmael Reed.
DESCRIPTION: Middletown, Connecticut : Wesleyan University Press, [2023]
SERIES: Wesleyan poetry | Includes bibliographical references and index.
SUMMARY: "This volume gathers Hernton's poetic work from 1954 through
    to 1999 — including uncollected poems and the complete text of Hernton's
    debut chapbook along with poems from Hernton's personal papers. The
    volume contains a chronology of Hernton's life and career, as well as editorial
    information with literary analysis and historical background" — Provided by
    publisher.
IDENTIFIERS: LCCN 2022056010 (print) | LCCN 2022056011 (ebook) |
    ISBN 9780819500359 (cloth) | ISBN 9780819500366 (paper) |
    ISBN 9780819500373 (ebook)
SUBJECTS: LCGFT: Poetry.
CLASSIFICATION: LCC PS3558.E695 S45 2023 (print) | LCC PS3558.E695
    (ebook) | DDC 811/.54 — dc23/eng/20221208
LC record available at https://lccn.loc.gov/2022056010
LC ebook record available at https://lccn.loc.gov/2022056011

5 4 3 2 1

Contents

Foreword

ISHMAEL REED

If the *New Yorker* calls me "fearless," it's because, like Calvin Hernton, I had been a member of Umbra. We didn't mince words, following the lead of Chester Himes, John O. Killens, and John A. Williams.

Each week we tried to out-blunt each other.

Calvin and I were close. We used to hang out a lot. He had a touch of the meshuggeneh. One day, I took him into one of my favorite bars, the 55, owned by Brad Cunningham, one of the first people I met when I visited New York for a weekend and decided to return to live there. Calvin started screaming. I told the bartender that Calvin was a genius. He said, "Take your genius out of here."

One night we'd had too much to drink. I dared Calvin to jump into the Hudson River. He jumped in. A cop wanted to take him to Bellevue, a hospital that included treatment for mental illness. I had to convince the cop that it was a stunt. According to the *Village Voice*, we were lucky because the NYPD is instructed to fill quotas by arresting as many Black and Brown men as possible.

In 1965, I took Calvin to a party at Norman Mailer's house. The party celebrated boxer Jose Torres's victory at Madison Square Garden. He kept dancing with my girlfriend at the time. After each dance, he asked me if it was okay if he had another dance. What was I supposed to say? I was in awe of Archie Moore, who was present. After I left, Calvin and Mailer had an encounter. Mailer recounted the encounter in his novel *The American Dream*. Calvin is called Shango.

One day in 1965, Calvin, Duncan Roundtree, and I were walking down the street when I saw a cop leaving Mickey Ruskin's Annex bar carrying a bag. The *Times* was running a series about NYPD cops "taking bribes at low places." I whispered the phrase to Duncan and Calvin. The cop heard me. He was a real psycho. He took us to jail. Our friends bailed us out the next day. The cop had come to my cell on the day of the arrest. This time he had his Henry Jekyll on. He said if I pled guilty, I'd only have to spend a weekend at Rikers Island, which has such a history of prisoner abuse, and even murders, that they're closing it. This is the kind of deal offered to thousands of poor people daily, whether they are guilty or not. I said I'd get a lawyer.

The case was postponed for months. Roundtree and Calvin were removed from the case because the cop wanted me. He tried to destroy my life because I called him out on a low-life deed. I testified and pointed to the cop and his partner, who were smirking and glaring at me like two fucking goofy idiots, as having taken me to the station where the crazy one punched me. I kept talking with the encouragement of the Blacks and Puerto Ricans in the courtroom. I was found guilty, but instead of giving me a sentence, the judge just about ran from the courtroom. My lawyer said he'd never seen anything like it.

In 1965, Calvin and I decided that we would go to England. I backed out. I told an audience that I wanted to go into exile in my own country. An audience member got me a job teaching in Seattle. Calvin made the trip. He wrote about it in his surrealist novel *Scarecrow*. Doubleday was unable to sell it. I bought the remainders and sold them over ten years.

I settled on the West Coast and didn't return to New York until 1969, my last period of living in New York. Calvin was in England collaborating with psychologist R. D. Laing. I ran into him once when he came home. He was referring to bars as "pubs" and had an accent. I published his book *Medicine Man* and arranged for a party for the book, which brought out Black and white celebrities. The last time I saw Calvin was when I heard him read from the manuscript of *Red Crab Gang and The Black River Poems* in 1998 or 1999. The event was held at New York University. I told him that I would publish the book.

After that, I'd phone him occasionally while he taught at Oberlin but stopped because there would be long silences at the other end. I spoke to him a few days before he died. He said he was about to leave the planet. All I could think to say was that his Joe Louis poem was going to be reprinted.

Calvin, or, as his students called him, "Socrates," was among the most talented, exciting, and charismatic American artists. Some have dismissed him as a performance artist or as a "stage man," as writer Fielding Dawson once called him. And he could be dramatic, as evidenced by his appearance on *Destinations*, produced by Powertree Records, a Black LP company. He was joined by Jerome Badanes and Paul Blackburn. Blackburn and I founded the St. Marks Poetry Project, which was established after I closed down a Second Avenue coffee shop where poetry readings were held before St. Marks. This was after a racist physical attack on Tom Dent. Another participant in the *Destinations* recording was N. H. Pritchard, whose reputation is reviving because critic Charles Bernstein cites him as an important predecessor of the L=A=N=G=U=A=G=E poets. Pritchard delivers a dramatic reading that dances off of the record.

Calvin, for his part, could have become a Shakespearean actor anytime he desired. Often imitating a Black preacher walking behind a coffin, Calvin would recite from Job 14: "Man that is born of a woman is of few days and full of trouble. / He cometh forth like a flower, and is cut down: he fleeth also as a shadow, and continueth not."

* * *

Calvin Hernton was more than a performance artist. He was brilliant on the page too, which is why I published him.

He was influenced by the scriptures, T. S. Eliot, and Langston Hughes. But there are some things about Hernton that remain an enigma. I was shocked to learn that as a teenager in Chattanooga, Tennessee, Hernton was a juvenile delinquent charged with breaking and entering. He blamed it on "bad company" and got three years' probation — in Tennessee, where they continue to uncover convict graves.

In poetry, Calvin Hernton dared to go where others were scared to go. No fudging the facts because of pressure from salespeople. That was Umbra's way. And now, unlike some of the other critics, who go for the tabloid parts, this book provides readers with the kind of serious grownup attention that Calvin Hernton, a significant artist, deserves.

Acknowledgments

We are grateful to Antone Hernton for permission to publish the writings of Calvin C. Hernton. We also acknowledge Calvin C. Hernton's grandsons, Tyler Kerington Hernton, Calvin Spencer Hernton, and Antone Christopher Hernton. We have done our best to respect the Hernton family's literary legacy.

We are grateful to Ishmael Reed for permission to republish material from *Medicine Man* and *The Red Crab Gang and Black River Poems*.

We gratefully acknowledge the Ohio University Libraries for material from the Calvin C. Hernton Collection MSS14, Ohio University Libraries Mahn Center for Archives and Special Collections, Athens Ohio. We wish to extend particular gratitude to the staff who provided us with digitized material at a time when the Covid-19 pandemic made physical access to the archives impossible: Erin Wilson, Miriam Nelson, and Bill Kimok.

Photograph of Calvin C. Hernton courtesy of the Oberlin College Archives. We wish to thank Ken Grossi for his speedy response to our inquiry.

David Grundy wishes to thank the British Academy for support during a postdoctoral fellowship, and to thank the University of Warwick.

Lauri Scheyer wishes to thank Hunan Normal University and her family for their support.

We also wish to thank Wesleyan University Press's Suzanna Tamminen along with Jim Schley and Zach Meyer for their skill, effort, enthusiasm, and belief in the value of this book.

Introduction

"This is my voice": The Poetry of Calvin C. Hernton

A POET'S WORK

Well into the twenty-first century, scholars — and more importantly readers — are discovering the full depth and reach of North American poetic histories that have for too long been subjected to misinformation, exclusion, and censorship. Calvin C. Hernton's is one of the many hidden stories waiting to be re-told. As founder and co-editor of the pioneering *Umbra* magazine; a participant in the Black Arts Movement, R. D. Laing's Kingsley Hall, and the Antiuniversity of London; and as a teacher at Oberlin College who counted amongst his students the poet Kate Rushin and the actor Avery Brooks and amongst his friends bell hooks, Toni Morrison, and Odetta, Hernton changed thinking and changed lives. Yet, though he was often at the center of political and cultural currents, his peripatetic existence — from Chattanooga to New York, London to Lund, Alabama to Ohio — has meant that he is often overlooked in histories of the period.

As a critic, scholar, and teacher, Hernton's talents extended in many directions. However, he defined himself first and foremost as a poet. Hernton's poetry, presented here in its first substantial collection for decades, synthesizes and reveals the contradictions of the life he lived. It is, on the one hand, exilic, diasporic, and international, bearing all the pains and joys of his voyages, his turns and returns. But it is also deeply rooted: in his memories of his mother and grandmother, of the charged environment of the American South, in the love and tension of his closest personal relationships. At the same time, were we to know nothing of his life, his work would still strike home. In the following pages, you will encounter Hernton's skill with the poetic line, with fusions of narrative and lyric, dramatic monologue and the chants and songs heard on street corners, in clubs, taphouses, and saloons; his musical ear, lifting cadences from spirituals and hymns to jazz, blues, and R&B; and his unique combination of philosophical reflection and a biting directness.

Hernton's work forces us to rewrite easy divisions drawn in the contemporaneous period, imparting a furious plea for justice smoothed over in the discourse of official poetry and the model of the "well-made poem."[1] It's hard to think of any other poet who drew on and cited as wide a range of figures as (for starters) Paul Tillich, Margaret Mead, Frantz Fanon, Billie Holiday, Richard Wright, and Walt Whitman. One could gain a history of twentieth-century political and intellectual trends from Hernton's dedications alone. But Hernton's poetry is no mere grab bag of influences. Rather, it is a distinct and achieved individual voice that deserves to be reckoned with the high achievements of modern American verse.

> This is my voice
> These words are my words, my mouth
> Speaks them, my hand writes.
> I am a poet.
> It is my fist you hear beating
> Against your ear.

Written when he was in his early twenties, Hernton's frequently anthologized poem "The Distant Drum" has become his poetic anthem, and it continues to speak his poetic truth. Where Hernton's better-known peers and contemporaries, from Marianne Moore and Joyce Kilmer to Jack Spicer to Amiri Baraka, questioned the nature of the poem, its meaning and being, Hernton's poem made its own striking contribution. "The Distant Drum" serves as an announcement of arrival every bit as audacious — and a good deal more concise — than the "Song of Myself" that Whitman had rendered a century prior.

As he recounted at a 1953 reading at Alabama A&M College, Whitman, along with Langston Hughes, served as a key influence on the apprentice poet.[2] From them, he adapted the catalog form, the attention to vernacular speech, to urban life, and to political justice. As noted in the most recent edition of the *Princeton Encyclopedia of Poetry and Poetics*, the poetic catalog "is of ancient origin and is found in almost all literatures of the world."[3] Hernton's catalogs serve as telling indictments of the horrors of the twentieth century: war, nationalism, racism, and genocide enabling his poetry, as Ezekiel Mphalele put it, to "vibrate as a language of its own, beyond the local experience."[4] At other times, Hernton takes a simple figure and runs changes on it like a musician working a blues scale, sparking reflections at once humorous and deep.

An experimental, existential poet, Hernton always retained a gift for communicating complex ideas, sparking deep reflections on identity, writing, and being. Often, his poetry was shaped by the political currents of the time, whose effects we still live through twenty years after his death. As Tom Dent — poet, activist, and co-founder of the Umbra Workshop — wrote: "Hernton's work stands at the very vortex of the explosion of black poetry in the Sixties."[5] Forged in the era of segregation, the civil rights movement, and Black Power, Hernton's poetry provides a trenchant critique of white supremacy, presenting the urban insurrections, police and Klan violence, and racism of the 1950s and 1960s in tones at once satirical, ferocious, and despairing. "There is blood on the totem pole of the western world," Hernton proclaims in "Litany in Winter's Garden" an early, previously unpublished poem dedicated to Richard Wright and printed in this volume for the first time. Like James Baldwin warning of "the fire next time" or the apocalyptic cadences of Hernton's poetic comrade Askia Muhammad Touré (Rolland Snellings), his poems unleash prophetic fury in the face of democracy betrayed: "yesterday's nightmare prancing in tomorrow's dream," as he puts it in "Blues Spiritual," a poem dedicated to Billie Holiday. Hernton also ambivalently engages with the history of Western poetry, from Shakespeare to Wallace Stevens, exemplified in his bitterly ironic transformation of Robert Frost's inauguration poem for John F. Kennedy — from "The Gift Outright" to "The Gift Outraged." Taking on the urban malaise and metaphysical speculations of T. S. Eliot's war-haunted metropoles, he transplants them to the spaces of the segregated South and the ghettoized North in ways that the conservative Eliot could never have envisaged. Instead, Hernton offers the geography of New York City as a geography of the mind: a city of sharp racial divisions and existential torment, beyond picture postcards. Hernton's social engagement also manifested in his attention to issues of gender. Raised largely by women, Hernton's respect for women was an important part of his identity, teaching, and creative practice, manifesting not only in his poetry but in *The Sexual Mountain and Black Women Writers* (1987), one of the first major studies to look closely at Black women writers, especially poets.

While Hernton's poetry was socially engaged, he was not a writer of agitprop or protest poetry. "Looking back on Calvin's work," writes Dent, "I am amazed anew at the breadth, width of his poetic concerns, his incredible energy [. . .] This creative energy flows into a variety of poetic functions: poems for fun, poems for preaching, poems for self-flagellation, poems for contemplation [. . .] Hernton does not always comes to us in his Sunday clothes, he wears whatever fits the occasion; the occasions are those of a spontaneous, inquiring life."[6] As "the poet in whose breast an agony bleeds from a / secret universality," Hernton, like another important inspiration, Richard Wright, drew on existentialism, fusing philosophy and politics in a vital symbiosis.[7] And at a time when many writers were expected to stick to racialized subject matter and diction, Hernton's multi-voiced poetry drew on his early experience as actor, playwright, and director to channel multiple voices. While deeply rooted in his experience as an African American male from the South, his work refuses to be tied to a single subject position. Hernton's dramatic monologues draw at once from Robert Browning, Gwendolyn Brooks, and the blues, all carried through on a variable free verse that sustained much of his work. Like the blues, Hernton's work establishes both a personal and social field of symbolism that resists systematic decoding. As Dent puts it: "Hernton's deeply personal, almost metaphysical alienation serves as the springboard for his vision of black alienation in America. [His] is a voice speaking on levels reserved for spoken silence, below the levels of logical, surface-level reality."

While Hernton's poems spoke difficult and often hidden truths, he was a popular poet in the 1960s. Lorenzo Thomas, another member of the Umbra Workshop and a leading poet-critic whose *Collected Poems* was published by Wesleyan University Press in 2019, recalls that, in the countercultural New York poetry readings of the day, audience members would crowd around the stage with requests.[8] Yet, although Hernton was well known and highly respected during this time, and although "poet" was the authorial role that he most fervently embraced throughout his career, his tremendous output in this genre — both published and unpublished works — has been woefully overlooked. Generations of readers know him mainly from a handful of signature poems and his sociological prose, notably the landmark study *Sex and Racism in America* (1965). This book aims to provide an expansive selection of Hernton's finest poetry for devoted readers, and to introduce new readers to a highly original poet deserving of greater recognition.

A small number of Hernton's poems — usually "The Distant Drum," "Medicine Man," and "Jitterbugging in the Streets" — have been frequently anthologized from the 1950s onward, but many more have remained harder to access. Following appearances in venues such as *Phylon*, the *Pittsburgh Courier*, and anthologies edited by Paul Breman and Rosey E. Pool, Hernton's first volume, the "epical narrative" *The Coming of Chronos to the House of Nightsong*, appeared in an illustrated edition from small press Interim Books in 1964. A landmark in Hernton's career occurred when *Medicine Man*, his collected poems (except *Chronos*), appeared in 1976 through the auspices of friends and former Umbra comrades Dr. Ishmael Reed, Steve Cannon, and Joe Johnson. Selecting from two decades' worth of material for *Medicine Man*, Hernton revised and reordered poems into a series of thematic sections: "Ballad Poems," "Blues Poems," "Four Poems, Seven Memories," "Other Testimonies," and "Blood and Ethos." Subsequent publication was more sporadic, due in part to his teaching commitments at Oberlin College in Ohio, where he taught for three decades, nurturing numerous students including novelist Tracy Chevalier and professors Herman Beavers (University of Pennsylvania) and Donna Akiba Sullivan Harper (Spelman College). Poems occasionally appeared in little magazines, but it wasn't until 1999 that long-time friend and fellow Chattanooga native, Reed, once again published Hernton's poetry in a final volume, the slim *Red Crab Gang and Black River Poems*, with poems concerning his battle with the cancer that ended his life on September 30, 2001.

Our selection in this volume covers all the phases of Hernton's writing career. Before outlining the work that follows and explaining our editorial decisions, we'll continue by offering some snapshots of Hernton's rich and varied life.

A chronology of major events in Hernton's life and career is included at the end of this volume, and a fuller biographical sketch is provided in "Calvin C. Hernton: Portrait of a Poet" in *The Heritage Series of Black Poetry, 1962–1975: A Research Compendium* by Lauri Ramey (Scheyer), who is co-editor of the present volume and another Oberlin alumna who was first introduced to Hernton by Oberlin creative writing professor Stuart Friebert. In this introduction, to suggest the breadth of this life and career, we provide some representative snapshots — personal moments that are also slices of twentieth-century American literary and cultural history for this poet whose life barely entered the twenty-first century. Born in Chattanooga to Magnolia Jackson in 1932, Hernton was mainly raised in that city by his maternal grandmother, Ella Estell, who had a profound influence on his lifelong respect for women. As a native of the South who lived in New York, London, and ultimately the American Midwest of Ohio, Hernton gained a rich perspective on human and racial truths and aspirations informed by his sociologist's training (inspired in particular by the example of W. E. B. Du Bois) and his deep-seated aspirations to be a writer (following the examples of Langston Hughes and Robert Hayden). It is not insignificant that much of Hernton's educational and teaching experience were at HBCUs (Historically Black Colleges and Universities), and even Oberlin College — where he spent the majority of his academic career — played a storied role in racial and gender history by being the first US institution to accept African Americans and women.

During the early part of his writing career, Hernton traveled between New York and the South — where he studied and taught sociology — was employed as a social worker for the New York Department of Welfare, and came to the attention of the FBI on the basis of his earliest writing. Studying for an MA in sociology at Fisk University — his dissertation entitled "A Thematic Analysis of Editorials and Letters to the Editors Regarding the Montgomery Bus Protest Movement" — Hernton was, as his FBI file reported, "conscious of the fact that the people with whom he is living and eating are alleged to be Communists."[9] His earliest poems were published in venues like *Phylon*, the journal begun at Atlanta University in 1940 by Du Bois. In June 1957, he met poet, teacher, and organizer Raymond R. Patterson when they gave a poetry reading together at Patterson's Greenwich Village apartment. This encounter formed the impetus behind a series of readings that Patterson would go on to organize in Harlem in 1960, using a contact list provided by Langston Hughes. This initial reading and the subsequent series marked the beginning of the currents which officially coalesced several years later as the Umbra Poets Workshop.

The impact of other writers — sometimes serving as his mentors, and some of whom he mentored — was a formative dimension of Hernton's writerly life and eventual career as a professor. At Fisk, he took part in an informal workshop held at Robert Hayden's house on Thursday nights — "from four, to eight, to sometimes a dozen people, all students, who gathered at Hayden's upstairs apartment, which was small and cramped"— from seven to past midnight.[10] Inspired by Hayden, he decided to dedicate himself to poetry, departing for New York because, as he later explained (in personal conversations with Lauri Scheyer), he thought all writers must go to New York: in this, his attitude was shaped by the example of the Harlem Renaissance. But he had given no thought to planning how he would live or survive, and he ended up sleeping in Central Park, his poem "Young Negro Poet" recounting the experience. the generosity of Langston Hughes was crucial in helping him get situated in the city. Hernton described "dropping in" at the home of Hughes on Sunday nights to receive the double nourishment of literary conversation and encouragement with a tasty fried chicken dinner, likely the only proper meal he would eat in a week. Hughes was, Hernton recalled, far too gracious to embarrass him by acknowledging that the latter always showed up at mealtimes. During this time, Hernton also met the teenage poet David Henderson, whom he described as a brother and running mate. Hernton, Henderson, and Hughes would spend evenings "laughing and talking and socializing till the wee hours in the morning, with the easy gospel of the blues on the record player flowing continuously in the background."[11] At other times, Hernton and Henderson would walk the length of Manhattan, writing on legal pads, sometimes barely speaking a word, held in "comfortable, secure loving silences in which everything we felt, thought, and saw was communicated through a certain look, gesture, aura, vibration."[12] With Henderson and Tom Dent, Hernton was co-founder of the Umbra Poets Workshop, a collective of largely African American poets — though meetings were, as Hernton emphasized, interracial — including Ishmael Reed, Lorenzo Thomas, Askia Touré, N. H. Pritchard, and Brenda Walcott, who established themselves as a vital presence on the New York poetry scene and anticipated the Black Arts Movement.

During this time, Hernton also began writing sociological and political articles for venues such as *Negro Digest/Black World*. In 1965, Doubleday published his sociological study *Sex and Racism in America*. Praised by Hughes, the book caused a furor.[13] Crossing the ocean, Hernton retreated to London for safety on a fellowship from the Institute for Phenomenological Studies: here he would spend time at R. D. Laing's experimental psychological institution at Kingsley Hall and associate with the Caribbean Artists Movement (CAM) at "a pub called the Troubadour [. . .] with people like Edward [Kamau] Brathwaite, Andrew Salkey, John La Rose, Efua Sutherland."[14] Hernton also became a faculty member at the Antiuniversity of London (1968), holding a workshop on "Writers and writing — or the dialectics of ungodliness" with "everybody reading their stuff, open discussion, and an occasional guest writer from the London scene."[15] He also traveled in Europe, spending time in Lund, Sweden (1967), before returning to the US to take up a post as writer-in-residence, first at Central State University, and then at Oberlin College, where he was soon appointed professor in the newly founded Black Studies Department. Hernton's colleague Friebert recalled Hernton, Audre Lorde, and Toni Morrison reciting Robert Hayden's "Those Winter Sundays" as their favorite poem during an Oberlin car trip, and Odetta and Maya Angelou surprising him with a giant pot of birthday jambalaya following a concert, with Hernton removing his otherwise ever-present shades to wipe away a tear.[16]

Shortly before his death in 2001, Hernton wrote to his old friend Raymond Patterson recounting a trip he'd taken to read his poetry in Cuba, "hanging out with Cubans in 'working class' (or perhaps lower middle-class), places of music and song [. . .] walk[ing] the night streets for a while," recalling "the hope, inspiration, and political conscious euphoria of the 1960's," and reflecting on "Cuba, the revolution, the 35 years of American 'Embargo' against these people [. . .] the vultures ('adventure global capitalists') circling the air overhead, biding their time." As a tribute, he decided "to read my three poems in Spanish, without English translation," evincing his continuing anti-imperialist commitment and devotion to the value of community.[17] It was the same sense of community and dedication to preserving the history of the African diaspora that characterized his illustrious career as a professor. Forging his own theory of African American literature and culture, when few examples were available, many of his former students cling to their class notes — even today — and found Professor Hernton to be an abiding influence on their own teaching and scholarship.

In the present introduction, we can only hope to offer a taste of this rich personal and literary life of a writer, scholar, and teacher. Suffice it to say that his dynamic impact was indelible on all who knew him.

THE SELECTION

This volume gathers much of the material presented in *Medicine Man*, a large number of otherwise uncollected poems from little magazines and other venues, the complete text of *The Coming of Chronos* (reprinted for the first time), excerpts from *The Red Crab Gang*, which can be ordered in full from Dr. Ishmael Reed, and a significant selection of previously unpublished poems from the papers of literary editor Dr. Rosey E. Pool — an early champion of Hernton's work — and from Hernton's personal papers at Ohio University. We have arranged the text in broadly chronological, thematic sections that encompass the different phases of Hernton's career. While first and foremost a poet, Hernton's literary career equally encompassed prose writing. In addition to *Sex and Racism in America* (1965), perhaps his most famous text, his prose includes a major feminist critical study, *The Sexual Mountain and Black Women Writers: Adventures in Sex, Literature, and Real Life* (1987), and a well-received novel, *Scarecrow* (1974), among a number of other texts. He also left a final unpublished draft of a prose manuscript combining history, sociology, and creative nonfiction: he considered this to be the sequel to *Sex and Racism in America*, written from the vantage point of more than three decades later. The present volume contains brief excerpts of Hernton's prose writings, including his autobiographical essay "Umbra: A Personal Recounting" (1993), and excerpts from "Les Deux Megots Mon Amor"

(1985) and "Chattanooga Black Boy" (1996), in order to contextualize his poetry and to provide glimpses into the integration of his prose style with his poetry and poetics. We are hopeful that the present volume will be followed by a *Selected Prose* in which Hernton's considerable scope as a socio-political thinker, storyteller, literary critic, and pioneering Black male anti-sexist can be adequately represented.

Our *Selected Poems* opens with "South to North: Early Work," a selection of Hernton's earliest published poems, first printed in venues such as *Phylon* and the *Pittsburgh Courier* and in anthologies edited by Dutch critics Breman and Pool, whose independent ventures did much to support the work of African American innovative poets at a time of intense exclusion and discrimination within the US publishing world. Hernton's "Statement" for Breman's 1962 anthology, *Sixes and Sevens,* is one of his most wrenching and vital reflections on what it means to be a Black writer. "Scars of oppression barb-wire my people's personalities like sword-slits in the profile. And I put it into poems. I try to make it come alive." Written while employed at a series of Southern HBCUs, Hernton's early poems demonstrate his engagement with musical forms — particularly the beautiful "Blues Spiritual" and "Young Negro Poet," a ballad poem that was a favorite of Hernton's teacher Robert Hayden. Visible here, too, is the influence of one of his most important mentors, Hughes, in short and memorable poems like "Remigrant," with its defiant refiguration of "Dixie," announcing Hernton's return South from a 1953 sojourn in New York. The clarion-calling "The Distant Drum," with which we began, and the existential "Being Exit in the World" and "The Underlying Strife" address the role of the poet, "a perpetual struggle, an eternal / Cause of the-People" seeking "the liberation of a wilderness dream / Deep frozen in a profit-making civilization." An early engagement with political themes manifests in "For Ghana, 1957" (first published as "West at Bay"), dedicated to one of Africa's first newly independent nations, and in two poems for Richard Wright.

"The Lower East Side and Umbra" covers Hernton's renewed activity on relocating to New York, where he studied, undertook social work, and, in his own words, "discovered just how hopelessly I was possessed by the desire to be a writer."[18] Beginning with his autobiographical essay "Umbra: A Personal Recounting," this section includes poems printed in the first issues of *Umbra* magazine and some of Hernton's best-known Lower East Side poems, presented in dynamic and dramatic readings at events in coffee houses, universities, and apartments: the ghostly, fractured modernist blues variant "The Long Blues;" the vivid Harlem scene-painting of "125th Street;" the bitter ironies of "Street Scene"; the existential-political meditations of "Burnt Sabbath," a reckoning with his relationship with his mother, Magnolia; and two lengthy urban dystopias, "Elements of Grammar" — presented, hot off the typewriter, at a Columbia University reading to a five-minute standing ovation from a crowd of 2,000[19] — and "The Gift Outraged," its title, as mentioned above, parodying Robert Frost's grandiloquent celebration of the pioneer spirit delivered at President John F. Kennedy's inauguration, with Frost's world of New England pluck and natural beauty replaced by the hallucinatory nightscape of Tompkins Square Park, a space of Holocaust survivors, surveillance paranoia, and marital strife.

Next, we present the complete text of *The Coming of Chronos to the House of Nightsong*, "an epical narrative of the South" dedicated to the white anti-racist writer Lillian Smith and to Hernton's grandmother, Ella Estell, who was, as he later put it, "my first and deepest influence, mentor, and teacher."[20] An ambitious, multi-sectional poem, *Chronos* is a dramatic monologue audaciously written in the voice of hundred-year-old white Southern matriarch Eleanor Nightsong, who reflects on the passing of the Old South from within the crumbling remains of a gigantic and now-deserted mansion. Hernton recalls the story of the poem's composition in the excerpt from the essay "Les Deux Megots Mon Amor" with which we preface the text. Having written its first section in a single night, "as if possessed," Hernton hurried over to give a public reading of the poem in a high-pitched, intensely dramatic impersonation of Nightsong's imagined voice. The startling impact of this debut reading of the text led poet Jay Socin to offer to publish the poem with Interim Books: it was presented in a beautifully designed edition of three hundred, complete with illustrations by artist John Fawcett. Unfortunately, this edition is now almost impossibly rare, and, with the exception of an excerpt published in Breman's 1973 Penguin anthology *You Better Believe It: Black Verse in English*, it has remained out of print since. It is our hope that making this poem available again will bring renewed attention to one of the major book-length poems of the 1960s. The poem resists easy summary or paraphrase. It is a biting satire on white Southern racism and a visceral reflection on the themes of *Sex and Racism in America*. There are echoes of the cosmological surrealism of Aimé Césaire and of the dramatic monologue from Browning to Brooks. The poem can also be read as a precursor of the more recent popularity of African American persona poems through authors such as Frank X. Walker and Tyehimba Jess. But the poem is almost completely sui generis: ambitious, odd, troubling, and compelling in equal measure.

Following *Chronos*, our next part is titled after Hernton's 1976 collected poems, *Medicine Man*, published thanks to his friend and Umbra colleague Ishmael Reed, and presenting a series of generally longer-form historical, existential, and metaphysical poems largely dating from the 1960s. These poems serve as a bridge between the dramatic impersonations and metaphysical speculations of *Chronos* and the polemical political energies of the poems that follow. The title poem likely dates from the early 1960s.[21] An extraordinary long poem, it reckons with memories personal and ancestral, the speaker staging a spiritual journey — drenched in the vocabulary of conjure, hoodoo, and other diasporic, African-derived religious practices — to the redemptive figure of the poet's beloved grandmother, indomitable in a rocking chair, "singing in that rock!" Hernton is likely to have read this poem at the launch of the foundational Black Arts Movement enterprise, the Black Arts Repertory Theatre/School (BARTS).[22] Its presence in such a context belies simplistic caricatures of Black Arts Movement writing with which mainstream literary criticism has been plagued for years. The poem is not overtly polemical or agitational, but it *is* absolutely political — as well as historical, metaphysical, and philosophical — in its subject matter: a compressed epic that balances personal enigma and collective memory, defining Hernton's poetic voice and his contribution to the canon. "Taurus by Aster Fire" results from Hernton's deep friendship with the older, Italian-American poet Ree Dragonette. A bold, metaphysical poet working within an often-male world, whose work, like Hernton's, has languished in obscurity, Dragonette collaborated in an acclaimed poetry-and-music recital with Eric Dolphy at New York's Town Hall in 1962.[23] Acquainted through scenes around Les Deux Megots, Hernton and Dragonette developed a deep friendship. As "denizens of the city streets, [who] lived day and night in the cafes, restaurants, bars, coffeehouses and nightclubs of one of the greatest and most horrible cities in the world," Hernton recalled, "we ran together, and as the saying goes, were thicker than thieves, [. . .] carr[ying] on a mighty discourse in and through our relationship and the poems we wrote."[24] Dragonette wrote a privately distributed book of poems for Hernton entitled *Shrovetide*, and Hernton's own poem "Taurus by Aster Fire" responds to a startling poem by Dragonette published in *Umbra*, "Buffalo Waits in the Cave of Dragons."[25] Playing on his own star sign (Taurus, the bull), his April birthdate, the festival of Easter, and Dragonette's association with the dragon, Hernton simultaneously stages an astrological bullfight and reflects on the Middle Passage.[26] "A Ballad of the Life and Times of Joe Louis" narrates the story of one of Hernton's "heroes of all time," boxer Joe Louis, focusing in particular on Louis's fight against the German Max Schmeling in 1938, a symbol of the fight for strength and dignity against domestic Jim Crow and European fascism. Perhaps more than any other of his works, the poem epitomizes his gift for emotionally telling dramatic narrative: a history poem with an oral storyteller's punch that gestures at street toasts, boasts, and film montage. Shorter poems in this section concern music ("D Blues" and "Fall Down," an elegy for Eric Dolphy), mental illness ("The Patient" — first excerpted in Hughes's anthology *New Negro Poets: U.S.A.*), and a recapitulation of the role-of-the-poet theme of earlier poems such as "The Distant Drum" ("Almost Sunday").

"Riots and Revolutions: From New York to London" presents Hernton's most explicitly political work. Written just prior to his departure from New York in 1965 and across his stay in London during the second half of the decade, the poems reflect on the urban insurrections that gripped America during that decade, along with reflections on exile and racial diaspora in the former imperial heartland of England. Often bitter, and at times despairing, the poems are also full of exhilarating verbal invention and read as calls to arms, reflecting the reality of oppression and the possibility of transformation, in which "the dynamos of oppression [. . .] are also the volcanos of liberation!"[27] We begin with an excerpt from Hernton's key political text, the essay "Dynamite Growing out of their Skulls!," printed in *Black Fire*, along with the essay collection *White*

Papers for White Americans, a necessary companion to Hernton's poetic work. "Terrorist," debuted at a poetry reading by Hernton, David Henderson, and Ishmael Reed that was advertised as "A Conspiracy to Blow Up New York," was published alongside a feature on 1930s radical writing for the *Carleton Miscellany* and in the Black Arts journal *Liberator.* Dedicated to "the four Negro children / murdered in Birmingham while / praying to God," the poem responds to the horrific 16th Street Baptist Church bombing of 1963. "The Mob" and "Jitterbugging in the Streets" turn to urban insurrection — particularly the 1964 Harlem Rebellion — turning nationalistic celebrations, such as the Fourth of July, upside down and appropriating the popular jitterbug dance in what is at once dance of death and act of resistance — a bottle "picked up and hurled [...] above the undulating crowd / Straight into the chalk face of a black helmet!"

The poems from London — "An Unexpurgated Communiqué to David Henderson," "Game Life" (dedicated to novelist Colin MacInnes[28]), and "Country" — serve as progress reports on the climate Hernton encountered in the orbit of the Antiuniversity of London and the Caribbean Artists Movement, working through alienation and affirming his commitment to politically forthright verse. "Oh, I am in this world without a passport to humanity!" Hernton proclaims. Yet, "every night [...] among the wretched / of the earth," the poet "plot[s] the downfall of empires." At a time when empires perpetuate their hold on power by other names and means, Hernton's poems are necessary insights into the ideologies of US and UK white supremacy: biting, alienated, funny, and defiant at once.

Our selection now turns to the work Hernton produced following his return to the US in the early 1970s. Soon appointed to a faculty position at Oberlin, much of his subsequent poetic work dealt with the social atmosphere and landscape of his adopted state, often returning to the pithy and accessible forms of his earliest work, with a new sense of poise that at times suggests the balance of Richard Wright or Sonia Sanchez's *haiku.* As Hernton put it, he came to view poetry and identity in terms of a "dialectic of Being and Becoming."[29] "The inner part of me has always borne a fundamental identification with women. Women are the people of my earliest memories, a house full of them," he wrote in 1983.[30]

"Low Down and Sweet" pays playful tribute to a host of Black women, as Hernton plays the dozens with Reed, repurposing the form from masculine aggression to joyous tribute. The variations-on-a-theme of "Hands" suggest Hernton's clarity, accessibility, and affection for ordinary, working-class Black people, "grown old now and standing / In a crowd among themselves," as "birds descend, swoop down out of the / Sky and slip up behind and cover the people's / Eyes with their wings." A series of Ohio poems, first published in the *Greenfield Review* and in Ishmael Reed and Al Young's *Quilt*, move from agricultural pastorals to the presence of the Ku Klux Klan, rowdy taphouses to the indomitable force of individuals. Tributes to three very different literary figures follow. A "Night Letter" to novelist John A. Williams reflects on the racist neglect of Black writers in the publishing industry, as powerful works remain out-of-print — a dilemma to whose truth scholars and readers of the Black Radical counter-canon can well attest. Another nocturnal dialogue — this time with Whitman, one of Hernton's earliest influences — is followed by a paean to Amiri Baraka, charting his move from young avant-gardist — the guise in which he first encountered Reed and Hernton at New York jazz club the Five Spot, a story on which all three writers have provided their written variants — to "proletarian cat" and Marxist activist.[31] Three political poems first published in *The Black Scholar* round off this section, paying tribute and solidarity to the people of Grenada, Angola, Mozambique, and Namibia, and lamenting the NYPD's murder of Michael Stewart in a vocabulary that channels the best of Hughes's Black and Red verse.[32] As Hernton wrote of Hughes in 1993, they offer "direct declarative statement, [. . .] the depictive cognitive symbol and metaphor in plain language."[33]

Our selection of Hernton's published work ends with excerpts from his final book, *The Red Crab Gang and Black River Poems*, which was once again originally published by Ishmael Reed. "The Red Crab Gang" sequence, dedicated to Groesbeck Parham, MD, the doctor who treated him in his final terminal illness and himself an Oberlinian and civil rights veteran, playfully refigures the cells attacking his body in a landscape that draws from the work of Amos Tutuola — a particular favorite — and a whole host of associations to do with the red color of blood. The poem is a reckoning with life, with poetry, and with the philosophical questions that preoccupied Hernton throughout his writing life, addressed with a humanist clarity and great poignancy. The "Black River Poems," a more miscellaneous set of poems broadly concerned with Ohio landscapes, are luminous, playful tributes to people and places. Echoing the blues, the last word is left to the all-knowing, enigmatic Black River:

Only the Black River knows
Only the river knows

The Selected Poems of Calvin C. Hernton also contains a broad assortment of unpublished poems. Though only a few are dated, most of these were written in the 1960s and 1970s, supplementing and deepening the range of concerns represented by Hernton's published work. Tributes to Hernton's first wife, Mildred, and mysterious poems at once existential and political, like "Black Metathesis" and "When Broomriders Black," inhabit that singular terrain — vatic, declarative yet ambiguous, and with a fundamental enigma at heart — at which no other writer quite matched Hernton. Pithy and memorable blues and blues-like poems like "Deep Sea Blues," "Id and Ego," and "Statement (For the Class of 1954)" have something of the quality of Hernton's great friend Raymond R. Patterson. The mysterious, erotic "Wooing of the Little Girl Who Lives in a Dark Hall" provides further insight into Hernton's poetic dialogue with Dragonette; the later poem "Hank Dixon and the Law" retools the badman and outlaw figure as fighter against racial injustice, turning ideas of "law and order" on their head; and "Mad Dogs in Vietnam," written in London in 1966, excoriates the butchers who sat in the White House, proclaiming death and raining down napalm on the heads of civilians.

This part of the book also contains a series of long, multi-section poems from across the 1960s and 1970s. Presented in typescript, often in several versions, with multiple hand-written revisions, these are not always finished works but are presented here in the spirit of works in progress, insights into Hernton's creative process and with many extraordinary moments in their own right. Likely dating from 1960, "Litany in Winter's Garden" once again pays tribute to Wright, developing the figure of a barren garden that at once evokes the parks of Wright's exilic Paris, the biblical Gardens of Eden and Gethsemane, the cotton fields of Alabama, and the horrific location of southern lynching and anti-Black violence. In Hernton's poem, these are spaces of suffering, death, and, in the poems' Christological vocabulary, of potential redemption, refiguring lynching victims as saviors in the vein of Hughes's "Christ in Alabama," Countee Cullen's "The Black Christ," and Gwendolyn Brooks's "The *Chicago Defender* Sends a Man to Little Rock." Another lengthy poem, "A Lantern for Abigail Moonlight," is dedicated to Dragonette and to Nora Hicks, a white participant in the Umbra workshops and first wife of activist and Umbra member Calvin Hicks. Hernton here takes up the themes of social stigmatization and the misogynist persecution of "witches," also explored in his novel *Scarecrow*. In the process, he riffs off Kenneth Patchen's visionary, anarcho-pacifist poetic novel *The Journal of Albion Moonlight* (1941), the Salem witch trials, and the McCarthyism of the 1950s. Hernton's catalogue of "witches," from Salem to Selma, joins together in a group as symbols of rebellion and poetic-political inspiration, transcending race, gender, and historical epochs. Our final selection, "A Canticle for the 60s," written in memoriam following Dragonette's death in early 1979, is a retrospective chronicle at once somber and jubilant, a sweeping landscape brimming with oral force and associative power. Here, poetry is chronicle, witness, and force of resurrection. For all the anguish, the racialized and existential agony that sometimes appears in Hernton's poetry, such work manifests above all the force of humanist strength and defiance that he learned from his grandmother Ella Estell: a belief that we can learn from and move beyond the ravages of history in what he calls a "dialectic of Being and Becoming."

> Joy you gonna see
> Joy you gonna see
> Joy for the dead
> And joy for the living —
> [. . .] Sing a song of praise, and do not mourn.

A NOTE ON THE TEXTS
In his half-century publishing career, Hernton treated individual poems more as elements in a traveling mosaic than as fixed entities. Unlike some poets who were rigid about versions, decisions, and changes, Hernton

was much more fluid. His revision process was a process of paring down to a poem's essence, especially in diction and verbiage. The revisions in *Medicine Man* tend toward compression and concision, as well as to historical shifts in usage: for instance, "Ballad of a Young Negro Poet" becomes "Ballad of a Young Jacklegged Poet." In some cases, Hernton was revising a poem from twenty years previously. In most cases, we've reprinted the late versions prepared for *Medicine Man* as representing something close to a final version, but in some we've felt that the more concise, writerly versions he produced later take away some of the oral, dramatic, and narrative power of earlier versions. Given this, we've opted for earlier published versions of the poems in question. All such decisions are explained in the notes found at the end of the book.

The unpublished poems we present here are taken from typescript, in many instances from a draft state with extensive handwritten revisions. It is our hope that printing the poems does justice to Hernton's work and intentions. Our notes additionally outline places of first publication, significant revisions between different printed versions of a poem, information on the status of unpublished manuscripts, and editorial decisions. The volume concludes with a timeline of Hernton's career and a selected bibliography of his work.

We hope that the book you hold in your hands offers a fitting selection of Calvin C. Hernton's poetry to restore his reputation to its past stature and attract the new readers that he so richly deserves, and that in it you might find his words living afresh.

NOTES

1. In this sense, Hernton's work manifests what Nathaniel Mackey, in another context, has called "a discontent with and a critique of the individual poem as a bounded, discrete, self-sufficient achievement, the well-made poem that stands by itself as if everything that needs to be in it is in it." Mackey, *Paracritical Hinge: Essays, Talks Interviews* (Iowa City: University of Iowa Press, 2018), 307.

2. "A PROGRAM OF POETRY By Calvin C. Hernton [Given at Alabama A & M College, November 24, 1953])." Calvin C. Hernton Collection, MSS14, Ohio University Libraries, Mahn Center for Archives and Special Collections, Box 2, Folder 7.

3. R. A. Hornsby, T. V. F. Brogan, J. P. Warren, "Catalog," in Stephen Cushman,

Clare Cavanagh, Jahan Ramazani, and Paul Rouzer (eds.), *The Princeton Encyclopedia of Poetry and Poetics: Fourth Edition* (Princeton, NJ: Princeton University Press, 2012), 214.

4. Ezekiel (Es'kia) Mphalele. *Voices in the Whirlwind and Other Essays* (New York: Hill and Wang, 1972), 48–49.

5. Tom Dent, "A Voice from a Tumultuous Time" [rev. of Calvin Hernton, *Medicine Man*], *Obsidian* 6 (Spring–Summer 1980): 103–6.

6. Dent, 246.

7. Hernton, "The Point," *Pocket Pal*, 2.3 (Spring 1977); not included in this volume.

8. Lorenzo Thomas, *Extraordinary Measures: Afrocentric Modernism and Twentieth Century American Poetry* (Tuscaloosa, AL: University of Alabama Press, 2000), 136.

9. FBI file for Calvin Hernton, accessed through Freedom of Information request by William J. Maxwell. *F. B. Eyes Digital Archive: FBI Files on African American Authors and Literary Institutions Obtained through the U.S. Freedom of Information Act (FOIA)*. http://omeka.wustl.edu/omeka/files/original/888ed4856f2b29648fd6d3659409c100.pdf

10. Hernton, "The Passion of Robert Hayden." *Obsidian* 8, no. 1, A Robert Hayden Special Issue (Spring 1982): 177.

11. Hernton, Letter to Raymond R. Patterson, April 27, 1984. Umbra Poets Workshop collection, Sc MG 538, Schomburg Center for Research in Black Culture, Manuscripts, Archives and Rare Books Division, New York Public Library.

12. Hernton, "Umbra: A Personal Recounting," in this volume.

13. For Hernton's account, see "How I Came to Write 'The Filthiest Book Ever Written,'" *Fact* 3, Issue 5 (September–October, 1966): 37,46.

14. Dennis Brutus, *The Dennis Brutus Tapes: Essays at Autobiography*, ed. Bernth Lindfors (Woodbridge, Suffolk: James Currey, 2011), 26.

15. Information from *The Antihistory Project*, a research blog collecting material related to the Antiuniversity of London and related initiatives edited by Jakob Jakobsen, 2017. https://antihistory.org/post/52398355128/.

16. Stuart Friebert, "Options: Remembering Calvin Coolidge Hernton," *Plume Poetry*, Issue 84 (July 2018). https://plumepoetry.com/the-poets-speak-7/.

17. Hernton, Letter to Raymond R. Patterson, January 24, 2001. Umbra Poets Workshop collection, Sc MG 538, Schomburg Center for Research in Black Culture, Manuscripts, Archives and Rare Books Division, New York Public Library.

18. Hernton, "Umbra, A Personal Recounting."

19. Hernton, "Umbra: A Personal Recounting."

20. Hernton, "Chattanooga Black Boy: Identity and Racism," in *Names We Call Home: Autobiography on Racial Identity*, eds. Becky Thompson and Sangeeta Tyagi (London and New York: Routledge, 1996), 140.

21. See notes for further details on the poem's probable dating.

22. Clayton Riley, "Living Poetry by Black Arts Group," *Liberator* V, no. 5 (May 1965): 19.

23. Thomas, "Alea's Children: The Avant-Garde on the Lower East Side, 1960–1970," *African American Review* 27, no. 4 (Winter, 1993): 577.

24. Hernton, "Les Deux Megots Mon Amour" (1985), in *Light Years: An Anthology on Sociocultural Happenings (multimedia in the East Village, 1960–1966)*, ed. Carol Bergé (New York: Spuyten Duyvil, 2010), 299, 301.

25. Ree Dragonette, "Buffalo Waits in the Cave of Dragons," *Umbra*, no. 2 (December, 1963): 46–49 (subsequently collected in Dragonette's collection *Parable of the Fixed Stars* (New York: Allograph Books, 1968).) A poem from the otherwise unpublished *Shrovetide* appears in issue 6 of Pete Bland and Tina Morris's UK-based journal *Poetmeat* (1964).

26. Additional poems for Dragonette are included in the unpublished poems section.

27. Hernton, "Dynamite Growing Out of Their Skulls!," in *Black Fire: An Anthology of Afro-American Writing*, eds. Amiri Baraka and Larry Neal (New York: Morrow, 1968), 101.

28. During the 1950s, MacInnes had authored a series of novels depicting London's emergent Black immigrant culture, notably *City of Spades* (1957) and *Absolute Beginners* (1959).

29. Hernton, "On Being a Male Anti-Sexist," *The American Voice*, no. 5 (Winter 1986): 74–101.

30. Hernton, "On Being a Male Anti-Sexist," 30.

31. As well as Hernton's poem, see Amiri Baraka, *The Autobiography of LeRoi Jones/Amiri Baraka* (New York: Freundlich Books, 1984), 181–2; Ishmael Reed, "LeRoi Jones/Amiri Baraka and Me," *Transition*, issue 14 (Summer 2014): 13.

32. See Langston Hughes, *Good Morning Revolution: Uncollected Social Protest Writings*, ed. Faith Berry (New York: Lawrence, Hill & Company, 1973).

33. Hernton, "The Poetic Consciousness of Langston Hughes: From Affirmation to Revolution," *Langston Hughes Review* (Spring 1993).

South to North: Early Work

STATEMENT (1962)

I write because I feel I am being outraged by life. I am *alone* and I am *everybody*, I am God. And I write because I take God into my wounds and am afflicted by Him and am afflicted by all of the absurd suffering and senseless bedroom agony of the world; and I am so parturient with nuclear debris and soul deprivation, and I am going to human being always explode scrap irons of painful mercy.

There is no "reason" for the poetry I try to write; there is only *cause*. The deformed, put-off dreams, the mutant hopes, futile efforts, spent living and spent dying. To the best of my frail honesty I write out of a deep, human, psychopathic need for salvation or murder. Sometimes I get premonitions of murder. Death by hating and eating, generational devolutionary slaughter by mating and excreting. In the cyclops of human denial the microscopic beams of snake eyes thrash my soul into conniptions of the criminal. I love my country, I *desire* America. But why has she got to make me hate her too! God is an outlaw. HE is me and my people; and poetry is the innovated strategy and the native idiom of my struggle for self-esteem and self-destruction among Others on an atlas board rounded not enough for black or white men and women to share one bed, or one grave.

Negro or "nigger," it is all the same. *Homo Sapiens* deformed by crossed sticks, corpulent green backs and the myth of white woman. Meshes of my psyche boomerang with centuries of sea-weed. Scars of oppression barb-wire my people's personalities like sword-slits in the profile.

And I put it into poems. I try to make it come alive. Because being Negro in the world, and especially in America, is to screw yourself perpetually in public. With black phallus jammed into your anus and white world cajoling supplication, deriding and demanding and defining it, you clandestinely emanate yourself a sort of God, a real God, but a deformed

God. And if white woman or man does not crucifix you every eon of your life, you do it to yourself anyway. And guffawing like that trumpet blower, with a million flood lights upon you, in the invisible darkness, you suffer something terrible.

And I am not resigned. Because, mainly, I am compelled to ejaculate it, to affirm it. And I want to be loved, esteemed and appreciated by the human race like anybody else does.

Remigrant

Been up North!
Chicago, New York, Detroit —
Up North:
Bright lights, fine women —
Up North:
Ride anywhere I please,
Get any job I want (if I'm "qualified") —
Up North:
All men, free men, almost.

But I'm back down home now,
Back down South — to stay.
Down South:
Black man, downtrodden man,
Down South:
Human freedom, taboo —
Down South:
I'll make my stand
As a human being,
As a Black man.

*   *   *

The Underlying Strife

If a poet could latch on to the word,
The word indisputable which is more
Than a transient thing —
If a poet could latch on
One little gesture, so slight a sigh might set
The strife in order.

But what is a poet?

A poet is not a holiday.
A poet is not a plaything.
A poet is a perpetual struggle, an eternal
Cause of the people
Towards the liberation of a wilderness dream
Deep frozen in a profit-making civilization.

Lord, if I am not a poet
Why are my hands so bloody!

* * *

The Distant Drum

I am not a metaphor or symbol.
This you hear is not the wind in the trees.
Nor a cat being maimed in the street.
I am being maimed in the street
It is I who weep, laugh, feel pain or joy.
Speak this because I exist.
This is my voice
These words are my words, my mouth
Speaks them, my hand writes.
I am a poet.
It is my fist you hear beating
Against your ear.

* * *

For Ghana, 1957

The hand who ravished a continent
Lies upon the map like a hoodlum's palm
Full of cuts and scars.

False gods are falling.
Tombstones standing where kings once stood.

Thou who hung on Calvary won't hang anymore!

I say I seek a dark continent rising across the ocean.
I see a sun falling back into the sea.
I see a moon going down in the west,
Dripping blood,
Like a predatory bird with a hole in its breast.

* * *

Blues Spiritual

For Billie Holiday

Midnight tears and the strange hurt of sorrow.
Yesterday's nightmare prancing in tomorrow's dream.
And today looms but the painful weariness of living
Mixed up with the restless fear of dying.

My grandmother told me
The slaves used to weep and mourn
Among the Alabama cotton fields when the noon-day
Sun was hotter than a fiery furnace!

Lord . . . Lord . . . Lord.

What makes a blues singer sing the blues?
It must be trouble
                deep
                    down
                        in her soul.

Richard Wright [1]

No man shall write my epitaph.
Dead men before me, live men coming after,
None have suffered the agony —
In Mississippi, England, Paris, Africa,
Along the streets of Madrid, among the tenement
Ghettoes of Chicago, within the blasphemed cities
Of Mecca and Bandung, everywhere:
Being black in the world made me the world's flame
The feculent kingdoms built on Caucasian supremacy
Are ablaze with the indefatigable furies of my words.
And no man shall write my epitaph.

No man shall write my epitaph.
For death is not the end of breath;
Project-wise, all men dead or living move in
That eternal direction of the immaculate vision
That is the star of destiny glimmering within the
Dark cave of heritage.
Everyman is an alien, a terrible knight inextricably
Strapped to a horse of flame that rides down a thorned
Path into eternal healing and burning light.

No — no man shall write my epitaph.
Though death rises like walls of bigotry,
The knuckles of steel will never bend,
The dynamite of blackness explodes the pit
Beyond my grave —
Oils of earth shake the foundation of the universe,
Marrow of dead bones sets fires revolving in the sea,
Cracks open the sky, and flaming floods rain down
To kiss my face eternally —
No man shall write my epitaph.

Richard Wright [2]

Mississippi
Chicago
New York
Paris, London, Madrid, Stockholm
Ghana
Mecca
Bandung
Dakar
Hawk!
Hawk!
Hawk!

* * *

Being Exit in the World

Being exit in the world
Is all over my hands
In my mouth, hair
Like syrup
Being absurd in the world sticks between
My fingers, and webs them.

Man cycled and ethos lorned
Exit in the hole alone I defend it,
I make it come alive, I come alive, explode.
I fill it with my substance, my finger, tongue,
Tears, anything.

Void in the world I exist.
All the crevices of life are meat tight
With the heat of my sweat,
I abandon none; yet abandoned am I
Alienated as at first sea eye keys unlocked

Fish hook from earth worm.
I am every project I fill, every mouth of food
Is my being in every body;
And being exits me, rots root and tree top,
My essence visits a million dark rooms

Pulsing, I lie naked with sleepers;
I choose them into being —
It is my ecstasy,
I am the leper who suffers to be.

*   *   *

The Wall

Wall
They were driven everywhere
And always from there were ghosts

She said stroke the tiger's bladder
Wait until April rolls down that river
And sing Where O Where O

Whispering in darkness they say
The wall crumble into broken clocks
The un-make-up mind continued making speeches

She said sweetheart I love that naked desperado
Where O Where O

Wall!
And they were driven everywhere.

Feeling

Sometimes I wish I
Had wings
Sometimes I don't

Sometimes I'd like to
Fly among stars
Other times I want to
Wallow in the dirt.

＊　＊　＊

Blues for Handy

In Memphis town
In Memphis he was born
Bright was the color of his eyes
Dark was his skin
And dark skin was a shame —
W. C. Handy be his name.

    Oh Blues, Oh Beale Street Blues!

He took teardrops and made them into notes
He took suffering and made it mellow in a Negro's throat
Sorrows that were worn and dreams that were torn,
He took the broken hopes of Beale Street
And made them sweet in a sighing horn.

    Oh Blues, Oh Evening Sun Down Gone.

In Memphis
In Memphis town he was born
But the Blues was a haunting theme
And made him roam in search of dreams

Dreams to light the dark that came over his eyes
Dreams that flamed the skies when he lay down and died;
Then stars were his eyes . . . then the world cried —
Dark skin no longer a shame:
The Blues had brought W. C. Handy fame.

*   *   *

Young Negro Poet

Young Negro poet
came from 'way down South,
Tennessee, to be exact,

       thought he had some verse,
       thought he could write,
       real well
       as a matter of fact.

Young Negro poet
came from 'way down South,
up North,
New York City,

       couldn't write so well,
       folks back home had lied —
       what a pity, what a pity.

Young Negro poet
came from 'way down South
just to sleep on the cold ground,
Central Park,
to be exact . . .

       Wake up o jack-legged poet!
       Wake up o dark boy from 'way down South!

Wake up out of Central Park, and walk
        through Harlem Street.

Walk down Seventh Avenue, Eight,
Madison, Lenox, and St. Nicholas,

walk all around —
        it's morning in Harlem.

Wake up jack-legged poet!
Wake up dark boy from 'way down South!
Wake up out of Central Park –
wash your face in the fountain water,
take a long stretch,
light a cigarette butt, and walk defiantly

    through the streets of Harlem Town.

The Lower East Side and Umbra

Physically, as a cohesive, functioning group, Umbra existed for only a couple of years. But in terms of its impact on my work and my life, the two years of Umbra's physical existence constituted a lifetime; its influence on my writing and its meaning for my life through the years are immeasurable and timeless.

I love everything about Umbra. I love the outlandish parties we gave to raise funds to publish the *Umbra* magazine and to keep ourselves going. But the three things I love and now cherish most are the writing workshop sessions, the poetry readings, and the friendships and camaraderie.

I first went to New York the summer after my second year at Talladega College in Alabama. From then on I returned during summers throughout my undergraduate and graduate years in school. After getting my master's degree from Fisk University in Nashville, I returned to New York and lived on St. Nicholas Avenue near West 119th Street in Harlem for about two years. Then I left New York, returned to the South, and spent four years as an instructor of social science in four different Negro colleges.

Unable to survive in those environments, I came back to New York, not quite knowing what I was going to do, except to find a job quickly. I had gotten married down south, and my wife Mildred returned with me. We left our baby son Antone with his maternal grandmother in South Carolina. I was unable this time to find a suitable place for us in Harlem, but a friend, Raymond Patterson, directed us to the landlord of his former apartment on East 6th Street between First and Second Avenues. This was how I came to be on the Lower East Side of New York around the beginning of the 1960s.

From 14th Street to Houston and from 3rd Avenue to Avenue D, the neighborhood was occupied with first, second, and even third generations of European immigrants, including Italians, Poles, Hungarians, Germans, and Jews from the Soviet Union and the East European Diaspora. Recently, however the neighborhood had witnessed an influx of young new-generation artists and artist types, beatniks and, later on hippies, including a great many poets and writers — Allen Ginsberg, Gregory Corso, Joel Oppenheimer, Jack Kerouac, Ed Sanders, and others — who quickly established themselves, creating their own spaces in certain bars and coffeehouses where they gathered to read their works, exchange ideas, and socialize. One such coffeehouse was Les Deux Megots. I found it quite accidentally around the corner from my house, which was on East 7th Street. I started hanging out there and participating in the poetry readings. It was the only such place where one of the owners was a black man. But very few blacks were there; often I was the only one. On one occasion, though, another black poet, David Henderson, appeared and read his poems.

I had been writing since I entered college, and one of my poems had been published in a professional journal during my junior year. Some of my professors, particularly my writing professor, had been instrumental in bringing me as a promising writer to the attention of Langston Hughes, at whose house on East 127th Street in Harlem I was not a stranger.

When Mildred and I moved to New York that fateful summer of 1961, neither of us realized the extent to which writing was a part of my blood. However, once on the Lower East Side, which became known as the "East Village," and having met David Henderson, my wife and I soon discovered just how hopelessly I was possessed by the desire to be a writer.

Recklessly and excitedly I gave myself to writing and the life it entailed. I hurt some people I loved. I hurt Mildred. I knew she suffered. But I pressed forward, relentlessly.

I do not recall it being so much a matter of determination. It was rather that I was caught up in something so powerful in me that it overwhelmed and challenged me, and I loved it and could not let go. It was living on the Lower East Side and getting involved with Umbra that brought this to a head.

Although Raymond Patterson no longer lived on the Lower East Side, it was he who gave my name to Tom Dent who, in turn, left a message for me at Les Deux Megots. Tom's idea was that the blacks on the Lower East

Side were very few in number — particularly the writers and artists — and we should do something about the isolation and anonymity we felt. We could at least come together and get to know each other. Tom said he knew several more blacks in the neighborhood — he mentioned Calvin Hicks, a political ideologue — and I mentioned David Henderson, the teenaged poet from the Bronx who was virtually living on the Lower East Side, spending many nights with Mildred and me, and soon with our son Antone and Mildred's oldest sister Pearl, both of whom had recently come from South Carolina to share our tiny Lower East Side apartment.

The first meeting was at Tom Dent's apartment. At the time Tom was Publicity Director for the NAACP's Legal Defense Fund. I do not recall how many people were cramped into the small rooms, although one (the "living room") was larger than the other (the "kitchenette"). I do recall, however, that at subsequent meetings dozens of us packed ourselves into those two rooms at 214 East 2nd Street. In the second issue of *Umbra*, our magazine, the membership of the Umbra Workshop numbered some thirty-odd people, including the founding members of the Society of Umbra, the first three being co-editors of the magazine as well — Tom Dent, David Henderson, Calvin Hernton, Ishmael Reed, Rolland Snellings (Askia Muhammad Touré), Oliver Pitcher, Lorenzo Thomas, Maryanne and Lennox Raphael, along with Alvin Simon, Nora Hicks (secretary), Norman Pritchard, Jr. (treasurer), Charles Patterson (circulation manager), William E. Day (production editor), and other members, such as Art Berger, Jane Logan, Mildred Hernton, Brenda Walcott, and the rest.

From the very first, the workshop sessions — where we read and criticized each other's writings — captivated, inspired, and invigorated me. The workshops convened on Friday evenings. They began about eight and lasted often past midnight, sometimes until one or two in the morning, after which we would rejoin at our adopted local bar — Stanley's on East 12th Street and Avenue B — where discussions would continue until Stanley closed the place up, announcing, "Time! — Gentlemen!"

The workshops and discussions were exacting, exhausting, and challenging. On any particular Friday night, if you were the twenty-first person in the room to read your work, it meant that you had to sit through freewheeling comments of twenty very perceptive and candid critics.

Nobody was spared. If your skin were thin, you were sure to bleed at some point or other: You would get angry, defensive, and you might depart just short of physical combat. But when you returned for the next session, your revised work was markedly improved, you were praised, and you felt good. You knew you shared in the criticism that contributed to the work's improvements. It was through these workshops and the Umbra readings that some of the outstanding African American poets and writers of the last half of the twentieth century came into their own.

* * *

I was proud to be a part of Umbra and the Lower East Side. The thrill of the readings would send chills up my spine. We became famous on the Lower East Side for our readings. The sheer anticipation of the readings was invigorating and renewing — we behaved like a dynamic, well-rehearsed black arts poetry machine. The fact was we never rehearsed or specifically practiced as a group for our readings. At the readings, we would form a line across the front of an audience — in a bar, church, living room, auditorium, theater, on a street corner or pier — and we would just read without having planned who would go first or what would be read, without any prearranged order whatsoever. Poets, we behaved in the tradition of the jazz jam session; spontaneity and improvisation were our guides.

The uplifting and enjoyable thing was that Umbra consisted of people who were as different as any group of people could possibly be — in background, education, temperament, sexuality, color, talent, and flaws — yet we worked together like the brilliant colors in a kaleidoscopic quilt. Our fame spread outside of New York into surrounding areas and even other states. People traveled from outside of Manhattan and from New England to witness the Umbra readings. Among those in the audiences would be important poets, writers, and editors. Some of us — Ishmael, David, and myself — read on national radio and an NBC television news program, "SCOPE," that was telecast from the Lower East Side. We gave tumultuous readings at St. Mark's Church in the Bowery and at the Judson Church on the West Side as a benefit fundraiser for a worthy cause. The readings were so good that I developed the practice of never going to a reading unless I had at least one new poem. Often the new poem would be hot off my typewriter, making me late for the reading in order to finish it. This was the case with what came to be regarded as a famous Lower East Side poem — "Elements of Grammar." When I arrived at the New School for Social Research where the reading was happening, it was over, and the master of ceremonies, Wilmer Lucas, was just about to close the affair when he saw me peering sheepishly in the door. He waved me onto the stage, explaining to the audience that I had arrived at last. Hastily and nervously I read the poem and received a standing ovation from about two thousand people that lasted for almost five minutes. The same thing happened at a Columbia University reading when I read my hot-off-the-typewriter poem about Tompkins Square Park entitled "The Gift Outraged."

The impact that Umbra had on the Lower East Side was registered, in one instance, through and by the friendly relations of admiration that many of the "old folks" of European descent accorded us after a while. The neighborhood became truly a rainbow neighborhood. Many of the Umbra people became "celebrities." My poem "Jitterbugging in the Streets," about the street rebellions, was read and circulated throughout the neighborhood in *Streets*, an indigenous Lower East Side magazine, in which writers like Sartre and Frantz Fanon were also published. Actors on the Lower East Side — like Moses Gunn, Lou Gossett, and Roscoe Lee Brown — began reciting many of our poems in their performances.

We also reveled in the jazz that we brought with us — Archie Shepp, Cecil Taylor, Thelonious Monk, Bill Dixon, Eric Dolphy, Sunny Murray, Elvin Jones, and John Coltrane — in the Old Reliable bar, in Slugs, and in the Five Spot, which was already in the neighborhood before we arrived and where we, especially David and myself, would sit directly in front of the many horns of Roland Kirk as he played our unspoken and yet nightly request at closing time, "Round About Midnight."

✻ ✻ ✻

Eventually, we were outdone by factionalism. But before the deluge, Umbra pioneered and grooved in one of the great adventures that left its mark on the Lower East Side, and indeed on a national epoch itself.

Just as I loved, contributed to, and benefited from the workshops and readings, the pleasure and inspirational friendships and camaraderie consummated all that Umbra meant to me. I had experienced deep friendships before, especially while attending Talladega College and Fisk University. There had been Robert Rhodes, James Wyatt, John Work, Dametta Moore, Marti Smith, and Lee G. Pugh. For several years preceding the 1960s, Raymond Patterson and I had shared a deep friendship — it was my very first friendship with another poet, a kindred soul.

But in Umbra there were not only poets but other types of writers and artists, including painters and musicians. I discovered another trait about myself: I would rather be around artists — poets, writers, painters, actors, musicians — than any other people I know. I do not even have to like all of them personally. Thus, I reveled in the relations and camaraderie of Umbra. I am forever moved by the specific friendships with Tom Dent, Ann Guilfoyle, Jane Logan, Nora Hicks, Ishmael Reed, and Art Berger. Without Jane Logan, for example, my first and now classic book *Sex and Racism in America* would probably not have been written and certainly not published by Doubleday — and I would never have known and shared the professional and friendship relations with my very first editor, Charles Harris, the first black editor at a major American publishing house. Although David Henderson was the first person with whom I discussed the idea of writing *Sex and Racism,* Jane Logan was instrumental in bringing the idea of the book to the attention of Charles Harris, who was her boss.

More than any of the others, though, it was David Henderson with whom I enjoyed a running-buddy relationship. We accepted each other totally and learned from each other. Some people perhaps thought our friendship was a mentor-protégé relation. On the contrary, it was an egalitarian relationship of incredible empathic togetherness. Days and nights we hung out together. We might walk the entire land mass of Manhattan, pausing here and there, stopping to eat, to drink, and to listen to juke box music, or abruptly sitting down on a curb to scribble on the legal pad each of us carried on a clipboard wherever we went. We did not have to talk. That was what was so great — the silences between us, the comfortable, secure, loving silences in which everything we felt, thought, and saw was communicated through a certain look, gesture, aura, vibration.

Although Jane Logan was instrumental in bringing the idea of the book to the attention of an editor, David Henderson had been the first person with whom I discussed the idea which eventually became *Sex and Racism in America*. But before the idea for *Sex and Racism*, a small-press publisher had approached me and published my long narrative poem in book form *The Coming of Chronos to the House of Nightsong*, which was advertised on the inside back cover of the first issue of *Umbra* magazine. Then *Freedomways* magazine published a short story I had written years earlier, and paid me $35! Next I published two articles almost in succession in the most highly circulated black intellectual and cultural magazine of the era, *Negro Digest* (which, in keeping with the times, soon changed its name to *Black World*). Both of my essays were cover-story lead articles, and I remember receiving $75 for each. As a consequence of a poetry reading consisting of Ishmael, David, and myself (which we advertised as "A Conspiracy to Blow Up New York"), one of the pieces I read, "Terrorist," was solicited and published, along with works by such artists as Nelson Algren, by David Ignatow in *Carlton Miscellany*. "Terrorist" was a poem about the bombing that killed four little girls in a Negro church in Alabama.

The works cited above were inspired, written, and published while I was working with and enjoying the camaraderie of Umbra men and women. I might say that I was "condemned" to be a writer. Without Umbra, however, without the workshops, the readings, the camaraderie and love, without the Lower East Side, I would not be the writer I am today.

Ballad of the Shoe String Kid

For David Henderson

"A" Train takes you nowhere in a hurry
Starting at 59th Street you ride like going
To hell on a thousand wheels grinding in your mother's belly!
As you ride the clicking and the clacking
Comes a-rapping.

Time
Is like an evil woman on the "A" train
Time beats you down —
Know

If you ride, eyes of the bushwacker will ambush you
In the dark path between wellsfargoland
And the quarter of the blacks.
But if you *must* ride,
Wee, Waa! Shoe String Kid,
Ride on!
Ride ride ride like a deadwood dick come back alive
In the free world of west lost.

Is it true, is that you, writing in the sky!

Free World?
Who's free?
Saw your mother flying in the air
Lord, I wants to go
Shot your mother down with a rotten pear

Lord, I wants to cross over.

Let's take a stance
Before we get put through some more changes
Easy, easy rider
Let's take a firm sight
Before tomorrow becomes yesterday
Easy, my train's a-coming easy
When I ride.
Know
If you ride
And the sound of the train comes a-rapping
Know
And the sound of the cargo —
Blacker the berries sweeter
The juice.

Hi, Ho! Shoe String Kid.
Fast as the North Star
Long as the underground railroad
Uptown and down
Full roll gyrate boogaloo
Uptown and down
The "A" train runs on a shoestring
The "A" train runs on a G-string,
You wouldn't kid me, would you Kid?
The "A" train runs on a Soul string —
If you don't believe me
Ask your mother and die.

Why, I knew your mother before you daddy did
Your mother had a little baby named Shoe String Kid
Shoe String Kid was black and Shoe String Kid was green
If you don't believe me
Ride the "A" train and be seen.

Where the burnt dream deferred
Runs wild

Jumps into the lake at Central Park
And comes out Uptown,
In the black ghetto beneath Morningside Park,
You can hear the hoofbeats of the "D" Train,
The ghost train from fatherlands,
Passing under the black ghetto, leaping like a fit
To a ghetto just the same —
Anyone of these clowns can change his make-up
From Swatzberg to Jones
Get his bones lifted from marshmelon
To stone.

Is is true, is that you, writing in the wind!

Apollo, Daddy Grace, Pentecostal storefront
Hoo doo, mojo, obop, rebop —
Get hip to your trip.

Dhis train don't carry no saints and holy virgins.

Oh, dhis train!
Oh, dhis train!
Oh, dhis train runs on a BLACK belt —
Ride on!

Ride on!
Shoe String Kid Wee Waa Hi Ho!
Dhis train
Oh, dhis train is your main man
Your stick
Your big deal!

And what does this all mean?
It means you got to ride like a one-gun fool
And shoot twice as fast as everybody else.

The Long Blues

In sun or cold the weather picks scare-crow
        bones clean
I am tired of ghost-water and willow years
Tired of pawn-shop dreams
And the tumult of clashing swords
Locked in my jawbones.

So long I have yearned to shake the chimney sweeper's
Soot from the marrow of my mind
And sail beyond these cutting blades of that
        horror Othello knew
Sail beyond the sensuous strut of the sickness
        unto death.

I am tired of flop-house mean
And cream colored grins on suckersize fish hook
Tired of eye key shot wink, and pistols exploding
In thigh fleshed naked, greedy for the meat-eating viper,
Murdering love, mixing it with money and crossed sticks.

So long I have yearned to drink the lethal medicine
And bid these mad driving motives farewell!
Still I drink, and drink.
My body totters, it reels.
And with the long blues riding my back like a sweaty shirt
I strut my agony out the door —

Quickly, re-enter for more.

125th Street, Harlem, U.S.A.

For David Henderson

Out somewhere I know a street
In my heart I feel its bitter beat
Worn out shoes and dirty rags
Slick head men and pretty young hags,
Ever clanging traffic in my mind
And through my veins runs the blood of iron —
Nigger path, hang-out corner, number man,
Walk softly Pete —
Liquor joint, beer joint, by day or by night,
125th Street.

Into some dive I wander,
Brown's Bamboo, Silver Rail, Fantasia, Palm Café,
Mean, hurt, lonely, prone to anger,
Slow on cash, quick of thirst,
Walk softly Pete —
I'll kill the nigger who touches me first;
Up turn glass, in my throat
The rot of 125th Street.

Back into the street I roam
This joint and that joint
Black man at the counter, white man own,
(Black man a few, still what must
I do and where can I go
To escape this monolithic ghetto!)
Rich girl, poor girl, Spanish gal, ofay slick chick,
Where can we meet?
Liquor joint, beer joint, by day or by night,
125th Street.

Out somewhere I know a street
In my being I feel its suffocating heat,

Upon my brow the mark of skin
Schizoid — sham span of kin
Sets me aloof to walk this poverty of fate
From whose trampled down existence erupts in me
A boiling love and hate!

Downtown white people play
(some blacks too)
Wide lane, slick-paved thoroughfares
Showboat, Flower Drum Song, How Green The Valley!
Uptown black people pay
(a few ofays also)
Sugar brown girl in the alley
Bubblegum neon and processed hair
Fairyboys, doctormen, junkie, long slick limousines
The body smell of my woman, gasoline!
Civilization? Culture? Oh, yes I know!
Adulterated Muddy Water, hippie honky tonk
White madness in a black cinema show.

Why don't I get hip and split this town
Before 125th street gets me down?
I linger because I know
In every town there's 125th Street,
In my being I feel oppressing heat
Upon my brow the mark of Ham
Schizoid — Oh, kin span of sham
That sets me to walk within this prison place
From whose trampled down existence erupts in me
A mighty strength to conquer space!

Street Scene

I met my dream
Walking down the street —

    Hello, Dream!

Dream spoke back:
    "Go to Hell, sonofabitch!"

* * *

Burnt Sabbath, Mount Morris Park, Harlem

(April, 1962)

I

Prior to beginning was always
Prior to always was harassment
Always was contained in harassment
Harassment contained in always
And always was motionless except for harassment
Within and without
Except for genes of life
And genes of death
And the windmill of perpetual beginning.

I was wrought upon that hill that April morning
Thinking of you my mother
I mounted footfall of childhood
Shoe lay kneeled over in the pathway
Saw fishbone left there
Heard children seeking each other in the bush
Saw burn-out star on a beggar's face
Burning in my brain my own enigma
Coming down the hill merging me with death

And I thought of you, and longed for you, my mother
That April morning.

II

We are worried about being accepted by people
We are worried about being loved
Each in our idiom hold the nightmare of our singularity
In our hands and cry out to everybody we meet
This is it, this is life, this is love.

How shall one commemorate mother on this day
Send her portfolio of April
Hands flinging palms to ground
Scenes of feetwashing and betrayal and the wind riding
Anemic bones
Send her wishes from the putative father
Or, shall he send her tears, proclaiming them love.

III

Wretched child born out of wedlock.

In the beginning was always
Harassment was the infinite property of always
Harassment had a definite shape and a definite form
On the seventh revolution of the perpetual windmill
Of beginning
The infinite property of always froze to an unbearable
Temperature
The universe turned into a monolith of ice
The wind froze and spanned the cosmos like an endless sheet
Of glass
Still it grew colder until at last the ice everywhere exploded
Sending hot fire and debris throughout the atmosphere,
And it was a billion times hotter than it had ever been cold

Burnt Sabbath.
Burnt Jesus.
Come, I will show you Africa in your mother's womb.

IV

The woods of the trees of the field went forth
To stalk upon the sea
The sands of the shore rose up to meet the trees
As they came upon the beach

What it is to be born out of the womb
Stand away from flesh and look at it
Identity beyond ego
Force beyond motion
We complain
Who would raise ourselves by lifting the plank upon
Which we stand
Who are afraid to speak
And who speak because we are afraid
We who sit on committees
Fill out questionnaires, send memorandums
Through channels
Who beat one another with sticks that have
But one end
We complain
But we do not want change.

V

Sunday is time for testimony
I have come to the zenith to witness
The ascension of three dead ways
I shall never betray you, my mother
But I am harassment in lilac bud
Decay in order and change in law

I am the fourth way fell from convention to know how foul
This Sabbath called "Mother's Day."

Sequestered historic and alone on the heights
Of Mount Morris
An ancient bell hoisted skyward by rusted iron
A bell forever locked in time
Forever generation coming and going
Tolls no more tallying of days over the city
Now burning in the thigh fork of multitudes

Oh see women walk with pride in the swift
Rhythm of skirt tails
See varied carols of people
Milling around
Salivating the exquisite poverty of the human enterprise
Bought and betrayed with silver
Holding, administering, heaving it
Into the heart of man's eternal.

* * *

Hate Poem

All you make believe
Go out of your way
Oil over your figurines
In my presence.

I, demon, monster
One day a million psychoanalysts
Shall drop dead
And you'll be caught beating
Your meat in the black maria

Of ozone boxes.

Your religion is killing
Your myths are lies
I want more, much more than you possess,
I want more than you are capable of wanting,
Your "founding fathers" were not fathers,
They were peckawood faggot hoodlums —
Who ever heard of executing a dog
For socalled acts of witchcraft!

And how come you always hung-up about
This big burly gorilla abducting this blond
Off into his jungle!
And when all your brave and outraged Jack Armstrongs,
Armed with tear gas, forks, knives, hydrogen bombs,
Come out there to "rescue" the lily maiden,
She runs out to meet you, with hands waving:
"No, no, no! Don't harm him. He's a *nice* gorilla!"

Then you mutilate him!

Your sons are punks
Your mothers are george washingtons
On whistler drawing paper,
Your daughters are bulldiggers
You are ashamed of carnality
You are afraid of fucking
All you know how to do is lie
Cheat, and derange,

I monster, demon.

Elements of Grammar

To Little John

I

No stars fell on Alabama,
Georgia, Mississippi, New York.
The Lucky Dime Salon is around

The corner from the Brooklyn Navy Yard.
Stevedores, seamen, truck drivers, cockroaches,
Construction workers,
And other rough-faced villains
Drink liquor and beer and tell a lot of

Lies and a lot of truths
About all the different kind of
Women they done
Made love to.
With his testicles and penis and muscles
And elephant's hide
That fit slack in the joints

Man is a lonely animal.

II

Around the corner from Brooklyn Navy Yard
This is the way the world is.
If I were woman who walked with the gods
I would know that long before Bismarck
Black Tribes came from Africa
And made havoc with Constantinople
Sent the white-frocked landlords running for their
Lives into the Mediterranean —

If I were woman who gave birth to God
I would stretch my thighs

And give Alabama, Georgia, Mississippi
And New York
Some good pussy.

In the Lucky Dime below the deck
Is a jeweled throne
Around which the sea is served in
Formaldehyde hallucinations.

III

No stars fell on Alabama. None but
The dead living know the horror of Georgia,
Mississippi and New York.

At night where stars do fall, you can
Hear mourning and groaning — at night
By gold god of moon
See blood of scarecrow
Bleeding on the deck below:

It was early one morning
I was on my way to school
That was the morning I broke
My mother's rule.

WASN'T IT SAD WHEN THE GREAT TITANIC WENT DOWN
Sin and salvation
Seven comes eleven
This is the way the world is.

IV

Around the corner from the Lucky Dime
Salon
In the yard of the Brooklyn Navy
There is much semen on the ground
And punctured prophylactics decaying
In summer heat.

I give you Statue of Liberty
George Washington Monument
And the Fastest Train Out of Town!
All crows cock when the owl is blind —
Bullet in the night
A bomb, a knee in the groin,
Redneck cracker

Pounding thick muddy boot
Down on the belly of a black woman
Sprawled in the Mississippi gravel
Beneath a signboard advertising sun lotion
For the obscenity
Of America.
With his little wee wee tucked under
The folds of his flabby belly
And trousers bagging his rump
Screaming and raving about the purity
Of the white race,
I give you the cockroach of civilization!

V

Man is a lonely animal.

So we mill around down here in the Lucky Dime —
Construction worker, truck driver, stevedore . . .

RECALL

THAT SHIP TITANIC WHITE FOLKS BUILT LONG TIME AGO

SO BIG AND HIGHCLASS IT COULD NOT SINK

AND THEY LET ONE NEGRO WORK ON THERE JANITOR

AND THEN THE SHIP SUNK MYSTERIOUSLY AND THE NEGRO
JUMPED

OFF AND STARTED SWIMMING THE WHOLE WIDE OCEAN

HIS NAME WAS "SHINE" . . .

Up from the deck jumped the Captain's daughter
Screaming: *Shine! Shine! save poor me*
I'll give you all the white loving a black scarecrow
Like you need!
Hallucinations

Of Georgia, Mississippi, Alabama, Florida,
Detroit, Chicago, New York, Boston, Tennessee,
New Jersey, Louisiana,
This is the way the world is.

Wasn't it sad!
An iceberg
A bullet
The moaning and the groaning —
        at night
        by the silver of the stars.

* * *

The Gift Outraged

Moon out of orbit
Nightly I have prowled the streets of
My neighborhood
Encountering ragged cats who
Screech away

As I lean from garbage can to garbage can
To green light to red to yellow
To green again,
When, finally, in all the dingy windowpanes
Of New York's Lower East Side
Red dawn catches my profile
And plays it back to me like a galaxy
Of twisted mirrors.

Many mornings
I have found myself in the park
Circled to circles
Where piss-stained benches call forth zombie
Supplicants pale and dry
From Buchenwald, Auschwitz, Dachau, Austria
The Ukraine —
And stray casualties
From where discarded wine bottles are of more value
Than human life —
All, huddled together still in concentration camped
Aggregates,
Sneer at me and mock me as I saunter among them
Forcing tears down my throat;
Not alone for my disillusionments
But for the gift outraged in the archaeological
Ruins of their faces.

Mornings like these
With lust and hunger and a bit of murder
We call desire,
Famine of night drives
One wearily to the restaurant of another's bed.
He stands there droopy-shouldered,
Fists tight in the hole of his pockets —
He does not know whether to kiss her
Or knock her in the mouth;

He slips the blue sheet from her pale body,
She is nude;
He stares at her; he knows why she has
Slumbered all night in this manner.

Through a haze in her eyes open;
Her body moves; face comes alive;
Once more, though dimly carved,
The One sees lines of the gift outraged
On the frail structure of the Other's cheeks.
"What the hell are you doing here?" He hears
Her saying. "Where you been last two nights?
What time is it? You been with
Your so-called friends drinking and running after
Women.
You leave me alone days and nights and don't call.
I hate this neighborhood. There are no trees. The window's
Broken. You look like you've been in a harem.
I only moved over here because of you. You got
Another woman? There are no suitable children for
My child to make friends with. Every night the
Puerto Ricans are having a rumble. There are no
Trees. You don't give me enough attention.
Me and my child needs a husband. You don't love me.
There are no trees. What do you want now?"

Her voice stops, her eyes go out.
He can hear her breathing.
He takes off his coat, shirt, pants,
Shoes, socks.
Sits on side of bed,
Sweat drips from his hands,
He lonely eyes her down there where she
Gasps and runs like a waterfall.
He bends, letting himself hang,
And kisses the nipples of her breasts; he feels

Tension release her body; he sees her scoot down
Under him and make the Arch,
The Elemental V.

Mornings like these,
Having prowled the night streets of
My neighborhood
For fear of outraging somebody's nightmare,
Red dawn opens in the park on my swarthy profile
And awakens me to the foul taste
In my mouth.
Who are these people here?
Why are they so old? Why do they rush to
Broken benches so early in the day?
Why do they stand and mill around
Circled to circles,
And why are their glances so quick and
Guarded with rejection?

Is it because they know I am not from wherever
They once were?
Even though I am here, is it because
They know I am not wherever they think they are now —
Or whoever they fashion themselves to be?
Are these people on pension, are they rich, are they
Wards of welfare? What are their names?
And why do they huddle together, avoiding and
Scrutinizing the others who are sprayed among them? —
Especially the young mothers and their forbidden babies
Circled away in the amalgamated sandbox behind the
Barbed wire of mankind's most abominable travesty!
Their
Names are *Stanislaus, Witkowsky, Kropokin,*
Pappenfien
Mayapuchin —
Their names are nameLESS!

So *this* is Tompkins Square Park?
What am I doing here?
Am in in the wrong neighborhood?
Why does my heart bleed?
There goes Juan Sanchez imitating the ethnic
Strut of a stigmatic identity, leading a flock of
"Untouchables," the sting of marijuana flaming in their eyes.
Here comes Judy Whathername walked by her Great Dane.
Yonder stands a figurine phallic deprivation, in trousers
That fit tight in the anus.
(*Would it were night.*)
And it *is* night.
The figurine struts like a prissy deer through the park
From bench to bench, asking for cigarette,
Asking for match —
Matches syncopate the park like fireflies.
(*Would it were morning.*)
And it *is* morning.

I see the carpenter's mother who has crossed my path
During the night, pillaging cans of litter and garbage,
Now coming through the park, bow of legs and squatty of
Posture, bulging sack on her back —
The lettering reads: ESPOSITO! ESPOSITO!
She speaks to me for she knows me
And I know her.
(Companions of the same demons.)
She says to me: "Something uncanny is going on in
The neighborhood. All night I have been collecting
Microphones; in garbage cans, in litter baskets,
There are microphones, and there are cameras too.
I'm going to hock them, should bring a sizable sum
For my labor.
What is more, I discovered during the night that
In certain densely populated blocks the fire-plugs
Are wired for listening.

Oh, I tell you something sundry is
Going on in the neighborhood."

Then she sides up to me:
Last night I saw a flock of birds big as ducks
With sharp-pointed beaks,
Swoop down out of the black sky
And pluck out the eyes of One who too like you and
I,
Walks the night.
And when he tried to protect his sight, the terrible birds
Ripped, from socket to socket, his arms.
When that happened a thousand white sheets of paper
Littered the streets —
Documents, photostats, resumes,
Contracts, oaths, reports, decrees.
On some there were hundreds of names,
And all the papers were stamped: CONFIDENTIAL
TOP SECRET
and I am outraged because among all of these papers,
I did not find my name.

With that the haggard witch gave me a toothless
Grin
And, as one dead fish drops from her sack,
Wobbled off with the load of the night:
ESPOSITO! ESPOSITO!

So I sit in Tompkins Square Park
Circled to circles on days like these
Contemplating the paths that have led me to
This neighborhood, to tub in kitchens and toilet
In hallways,
To fish bellies and vikings and rented motorcades
Of Puerto Rican weddings that are a little too
Flamboyant, a little too loud and joyous for

Gothic-faced anachronisms that foliate the park at dawns
And never leave until nights fall.

The park is no refuge for a gift, a statue,
Of a man with finger pointed up to air
That was outraged before it was ever given.
What is the gift saying? Who is he talking?
Why does he have his *back* to the park?
COME HERE. LOOK AT THIS GIFT, AT THIS STATUE, LOOK AT
SAMUEL SULLIVAN COX!
SUN SETS ON THIS PARK BUT NOT ON THAT STATUE.
JUST LOOK AT THIS STATUE. WILL YOU!
LOOK AT IT!
AS THE SWIFT COURIERS OF ALL OUR DREAMS
LIFT IT UP AND SET IT DOWN
ACROSS TOWN
IN ASTOR PLACE WHERE THE *ENCYCLOPEDIA
AMERICANA*
SAYS IT IS STANDING!

Evenings like these
I leave the park and prowl the Consolidated Edison streets
Where One finds his way to the agony of
Another's delicatessen.
And she, a serpent draped around her black thighs,
Stares the One down —
"Where are your eyes?" She harangues him.
"What happened to your arms?" She cries.
"What have you been doing with yourself all day?
Why don't you get a job? You have not kept your vows.
What's that fish doing in your hair? I'm sick
And tired of being mistreated. I'm sick of this
Neighborhood. Where is my son?
Have you put the child in the hock shop again?
What's that fish doing in your hair? You don't love
Me. Did you read what the *Daily News* said?

Me and the child needs a husband, a home. *What's*
That damn fish doing in your hair! Why don't you answer me?
Answer me!"
But the One stands there, dumb, shoulders
Drooped over,
Stripped of desire, drained of hunger,
Forcing the dagger back down his throat;
He knows as well as I he is alone in the dark park
Except for the revolving light in the big square clock
Where the outrage is calculated,
And the moon mumbles Black Sonofabitch at him
Like that crocodile there, that hairy one on the barstool
With the mean, smoldering eyes.

The Coming of Chronos to the House of Nightsong (1964)

from "LES DEUX MEGOTS MON AMOUR" (1985)

This is the way the poem came to me. One night, in my small, tub-in-kitchen apartment at Houston Street and Avenue A I experienced a terrible depression, a terrible restlessness, and I could not figure out what was the matter. Then, suddenly, as if possessed, which indeed I was, I sat down, grabbed a pencil and began to write — in the voice of a woman, a southern white woman — "My name is Eleanor Nightsong," was the first line I wrote. When I finished that night I had written some fifteen blank verse pages, which was the first section of the poem, which was to have three sections.

I ran straight to the Les Deux Megots. It was Wednesday night and the reading was in session. Paul Blackburn, or perhaps it was Howard Ant, who ran the readings, gave me a place on the long list of readers. When my turn came, without any explanation, I read what I had written. I assumed the voice and manner of a strong-willed, white, southern racist woman coming face to face with a hundred years of change in her beloved southland. Les Deux Megots was packed with people standing around the walls and in corners. They cheered throughout the poem, laughed, expressed awe, fell silent, and gave me thunderous applause at the end. A couple of days later, a note was handed to me. It was from Jay Socin, who wanted to see me about publishing a book of what I had read. The phone number and address was on the note.

Jay Socin and Kirby Congdon were Madison Avenue "ad" men. But during the evenings they wore jeans and sneakers and hung out with the artists, for at heart they were artists themselves. Congdon was an accomplished poet. Their small press was called Interim Books, and they had recently published a book of poems by the Whitmanish Marxist poet,

Jack Micheline. Right away I liked Jay and Kirby, and they liked me, I mean, as a person as well as a poet. They were friends with James Baldwin and a whole lot of painters, writers, film makers, and so forth. I told them there were going to be two more parts, or sections, to my poem. They were delighted. In two weeks I brought Jay the completed manuscript. They published it in 1963.

The poem was a long, three-part, epic narrative. It was written in the voice and from the perspective of a southern white woman awaiting sunrise on her 100th birthday, entitled *The Coming of Chronos to the House of Nightsong*. "Chronos" symbolized the century of changes which had taken place in the south and in Eleanor's life, transforming the south and Eleanor herself. The entire poem, but especially the middle section entitled "Metaphysics of the House," was particularly influenced by the poetics of Ree Dragonette. So I had first thought to dedicate the poem to her. But, on second thought, I remembered having met Lillian Smith when I was a graduate student at Fisk University. I had seen Smith two years earlier at Talladega College where I was an undergraduate; and had been enthralled by her ghostly angelic appearance and demeanor as well as her words. At Fisk, she had canceled an appointment with the president, she told me, in preference to spend time with "the young man who wrote so compellingly to see me."

I had read Smith's "controversial" novel, *Strange Fruit*, and had been captivated by what I called a *third voice* in the novel. From about six to midnight Smith sat with me in the swing on the porch of the house of president Charles Johnson. She was the guest of the president. But instead of taking dinner with Johnson, she gave me the time. Our conversation was so moving that at one point we were crying. Smith had been branded in the south as a "nigger lover," for writing *Strange Fruit*, which, she lamented, was reviewed and talked about as a controversial book only, and not as a work of art. I had been deeply touched by the artistic dynamic in the novel, and, sitting in the swing beside her, I was so moved by her attention and honesty and caring for me as a potential writer, that I can still feel the chills that came over me even now as a I write today. So instead of Ree, I dedicated CHRONOS to Lillian Smith, and to my Grandmother, Ella Estell, I wrote, both of whom were "great southern ladies."

The Coming of Chronos to the House of Nightsong

This poem is dedicated to Lillian Smith,
a great southern woman and to Ella Estell,
my grandmother

*   *   *

Part One: The Legacy of the House

I

My name is Eleanor Nightsong

You who were born after the death of my youngest son, Bobbie,
       fifteen years ago, have never seen my face
You have heard rumor, you have whispered gossip, and you have
       heard folks say one thing and folks say other things
You have heard stories and various legends about this great
       house with its long line of ancestors, its ethos and culture
       and its many, many rooms
You have come up here on this hill and gazed in wonder at the
       enigma that hovers over this house
And I have watched you through my window, in the twenty-seventh
       room, a room from which I have not wandered in fifteen
       years —
You have heard

I am in this room now
Like a riddle abandoned in the middle of a hurricane, I am in
       the twenty-seventh room of this great house
It is night and I am alone

As I sit here, in this room, in my chair, I feel a terrible
       quietness stirring in my bones
I have not slept the whole night

45

I am waiting on dawn
My eyes are sightless and fixed upon my window
My hands are bone lean, they lay folded in my lap

My body, hieroglyphic and weather-worn, is fragile force
I feel sound, ominous like power without source, stalking
          throughout the rooms and corridors of this house
My face is furrowed, is chalk white, is chrysanthemum vulcanite

And I am in my room now
I am waiting on sunrise
Waiting on fire and water

II

I, Eleanor Nightsong, am God
This house, built by my father's father and preserved to this
          day by me, is my Rock —
And when the morning sun walks up this hill like a natural man
          and sets my window ablazing with the flaming serpent of
          creation
I will be One Hundred Years Old

Oh, praise the Lord!
Oh, praise my soul!
I am going to live forever!
This house and this land will stand against all change
These values founded on ancestor creed and God's natural law
          will never perish.
Oh praise the bones of my progenitors, lined across three centuries
          back to the pits of England, the siege of Cromwell, back
          to Ireland, to my mother's womb and dead fish bellies.

Like refugee ants, my ancestors came to this continent one by one
The wilderness rose up to meet them,
The savage tribes with their painted bodies danced against
   the sun
The sun itself was hostile, the extremities of the seasons
   swept upon them without warning
But my people — the Nightsong Lineage — were fired with a vision
They were superior people, they were the best of Caucasian stock
My father's father received his commission from the great Duke
   of Hamiltonshire
My mother's mother was of rich blood leading back to the Tribune
   of Richard himself
For miles and miles as far as eyes could see, their property
   stretched across the highlands of Georgia, as if it were
   never going to end
Slowly, by dying and suffering, by killing and sweating, through
   hard times and bull-dog persistence
The great deed was accomplished
This land was cleared and planted, cotton and tobacco were
   harvested, women were married and babies born
Season after season
Negras were imported and domesticated to serve in the enterprise
   of our building
And as nights and days exchanged faces, as mill wind turned
   mill wheel
The House of Nightsong rose
Stone on stone, this house rose like a fortress
Rose on this hillside to tower over this community in the same
   aspect as a great sentinel of the irrefutable stability
   of blood and custom

Yes I testify to you, the ethos of Nightsong rose, spread
   and stamped itself upon the Southland like the hide of
   a mammoth buffalo

There were magnolias, azaleas and honeysuckle in every garden,
        cotton blooming in the fields, fried chicken on the tables,
        peace, prosperity and contentment became the inherent
        properties of our way of living in the Southland of America

Oh, praise my bones!

III

I am in my room now
And it all seems so long ago
Yet, inextricably, the good days of the past stir in my blood

What is the soul
The past is a living thing —

Pigeons roost in my hair
Sparrows make nests in the folds of my ears, they sing there
The wind moves when I wave my hands
My fists rise in anger: stars go out, planets explode
My voice whispers a prayer: old men fall asleep, wombs of women
        issue forth lilac and daffodil

I repeat — what is it to be woman, and know the burden of being
        all the good things on earth?

I wish to speak about my children, my daughters and sons
        the issuance of my womb

I wish to recall my youth, the hot heat of men upon my body,
        riding me down to plasm and photosynthesis
The joyous, fulfilling agony of stretching my legs,
        the pull on the anal muscles
        the prolonged vaginal thrust
The mystic emergence of a head, arms, a torso,
        naked, slimy, filmy-eyed

the total body of a living thing oozing out of your womb
still strapped to your entrails
yet set free forever!

This is the way my children were born, one by one — Cleola,
        Jeffery, Horace, Brenda, Eleanor, John, Nathan. . . .
On and on they kept coming, one by one through the years until
        they were nineteen, and then Robert, my baby, the last of
        Nightsongs, the ghost, the mysterious scarecrow of my
        conscience
Oh yes, the guilt, the immorality
Should I have told him, ever should I have whispered in his
        ear why his nose was so broad and hair coarse and unruly. . . .

Oh planets explode!
Oh stars go out!
Oh pigeons fly in and out of my mouth!
Oh sparrows flutter and soar like jets in my womb!
Oh how the black seed swells in my loins, lifts me
        boomerangs my white flesh
Lets me down to serene disaster
Naked and complete . . .

Should I hate the soul
Should I hate lilac and daffodil
Should I hate the touch of wooly hair
Should I hate monstrosity
And should I know what it is to be lily flower and bear the
        burden of my fathers' crimes

I wish only to speak about my children, my daughters and sons
To speak about the indestructible glory of this great house

Hush! —
Who goes, in the dark of night, upon that lonesome hill!

IV

I may be dead before sun walks over the mountains
How does it feel to stand without and look on the inside
How will we recognize the hands of our clocks if they break
        loose and walk up to us and shake us awake!

The soul is more than a retroactive dream

That is the way Cyril died, my first husband, in a dream
That must be horrible, or easy, to die in sleep . . . dreaming
Or is it the inability to know how it is that makes it seem terrible
Dying *is* a dream
We believe our dreams while we are dreaming them

Cyril gave me five children, and I was thirty-seven when he
        sauntered into his dream that summer evening and never
        walked from it

I wonder is it still the same sunny evening for him
Is he still dreaming that dream, whatever it was

There was a smile on his face

I wonder if he was dreaming of the splendor of this great house
        the magnificence of the plantation
        the cotton, tobacco and indigo stretching everywhere
        the negras singing in the fields
        the almost endless expanse of our property where one could
        ride from sun-up to sundown and never exhaust this great estate
        the gentry and the eloquence, the magnitude of our social
        affairs, the lily ladies and wellbred families;
        the lean mulatto wenches in their huts, the one in our kitchen

Perhaps not! — for I discovered a trace of agony on his lips
        before he slipped into oblivion

No dream is totally *only* dream
Perhaps the nightmare of that war loomed in Cyril's sleep like
 a runaway scarecrow stalking the field Northward
 the iron-chiseled musculature of Abe Lincoln shouting
 down intrusion upon our way of life
 the dying and starving, the rape and pillage
 and that pyro-maniac general, marching, burning, collecting
 negras in his ranks, marching and burning
 all the way from Charleston through Atlanta, Mobile,
 clear to the Gulf of Mexico!
 leaving behind everywhere ashes and brimstone

Oh, what a cruel wrath!
Down from Chicago, New York, Maine, Boston, New Hampshire,
 the Yankee dogs came
 erecting schools, building churches, setting up ballot boxes
 promising forty acres and a mule to every black nigger
And the niggers believed, the stupid niggers! —
Like eunuchs suddenly illusioned with the dream of unlimited
 potency, the niggers ran from the fields, from the big
 houses
The darkies ran from the people who had loved and protected
 them; ran, screaming *freedom*; ran into the arms of traitors,
 carpetbaggers and filthy opportunists

Oh, how cruel the wrath!
The era of Black Domination, like a mammoth plague, fell upon
 the Southland
There were niggers voting, niggers holding political office,
 niggers governor, niggers senator, niggers district attorney
 rampart niggers prowling the streets and raping white women
Riot and Armageddon ensued everywhere

These were hard days for the House of Nightsong, for the whole
 Southland

But we were not put down for long by these darkies
A superior people, linked by blood and skin, will never submit
        to domination and tyranny
By the help of God Allmighty, the white people struck back at
        the negra race and their filthy consorts from the North
And, like a mighty white sheet, we rose up in one great Klan
We put the niggers in their places again, drove the Yankees out
        and established peace and harmony and democracy in the
        Southland once more
But Cyril never lived to rejoice in this
By then I was wedded to Franklin, a distant cousin to the great
        John Calhoun —

Dying and living are names for stability of creed and ethos

V

Hark!
My room grows translucent
My eyes feel the presence of the sun walking over the Blue Ridge
        Mountains toward my window
Soon I will be a thousand years old

The spectre of Bobbie's father keeps coming up

A thousand years old!
Am I confused
Am I confused

Jacob, my third and final husband gave me seven children —
        or was it six? —

The question of Bobbie, my baby, keeps plaguing my mind

Franklin was crippled in his left leg and walked with a limp
He was a silent, impenetrable man

And except in the act of love, I never understood him
Never took him totally

A hundred years old
Am I confused
Do I dare tread rays of light to where clocks of heritage
        click off Neptune and the sovereign rights of states

What is it to be woman, sweet loving and senile, in the world
        of men
I fight for my young,
Like a tigress, a woman puts her young before all,
        before husband, brother, mother
        before hell or values of society —

Who, among men, knows what a woman feels when a living animal
        leaps from her private, innermost organs
Who goes up on that lonesome hill!

And do I dare disturb petrified pontifications of artifact
        and museum
And am I confused
Do I hesitate like the sun, my twin, at morning-tide
And what is it to pass age into centennial
Living and dying are violets for the indestructible solidification
        of past, present, and future.

VI

A person does not change overnight
A person, depending on the manners he is raised up with
        and the folklore of his natural race —
A person cannot relinquish, cannot make anarchy with what
        anchors his true nature and validates his reasons for
        existing and self-esteem
Human nature is the same and will always be the same

No person really ever changes
So is it, I say, with nations, cults, tribes, societies

And I am not undecided

God made night one day and made day the other day
Segregation is the natural order of peace and harmony
Fowl, floral, rock, water, fire
These elemental as day and night
And in all things, we, the colored and white races of the South
       will work together like hands
Separated like fingers!

Am I confused
Living and dying
Do I dare
Growing and decaying

Upon my limbs I restored and lifted this house and its ethos
       to the present status quo of its status
Nothing has changed, nothing will change
By my limbs, no court, no communist negra organization, no
       god or devil will force me gradually, or otherwise,
       to abandon the heritage of our Southern way of life
       which is just and most democratic

And I am not confused
I am not confused
And I do, indeed, dare

The negras are an inferior race
The negras are black
The negras are prone to rape, murder, consumption, and other
       crimes of the flesh
The negras are born black and the white people are born white

The negra women have wide and protruding buttocks, and they
        eat their young
The negra men are black and snarling, and they want to soil white
        flesh of white ladies and make black babies in white women
Rage! O rage against the Negras!

And I am not confused

VII

Behold! —
The sun rolls upon the land like a ball of fire!
It is Nineteen Hundred and Sixty-Two in the year of my God
Allmighty!

Omnipotent and indefatigable is She!
Omnipotent and indefatigable the House of Nightsong!
Omnipotent and indefatigable the Southland!

Sing praise my bones!
Oh, I am One Century toward God and Eternal life!

Oh, I Eleanor, of Nightsong, am going to live forever!

Part Two: The Metaphysics

Elemental Century

> Taste of salt in the skin
> Time-anviled through
> A burning glass
> Visions hammered for
>
> Future generations

Elemental Soil

> Smell of tumor in the bowels
> Winged furniture
> Locked in memory
> Fire and water explode
>
> The hot land

And I said to my soul
Do you understand these violets
In the soil

> Idiomatic protoplasm
> Through an ageless orthodoxy
> Etch nature's eternal revolution
> Humus and legumes
> Alfalfa
> Bits of information unclarified
> Undersea forces
> Chasms
> Break sky-shore
> Unlock fish belly from
> Earth eye-keys

And I said to my soul
Listen to these voices in the universe

Ontological dream
Diadem jeweled genteel ladies
Tomatoes, rivers of spleen
Ejaculations of an unknown perfume
Chiffon gowns calico and red
Erosion, texture of hair evaporation
The teeth decay
Halls lifted vertical
On granite limbs
Clods of southern earth
Menopause, flow of oil drop out
Dogwood, honeysuckle pollen
Magnolia fragrance
Splintered meteor
Particles coagulate, stratify
Splinter hurl
Disintegrate cycling

Century be still

Domino schizoid
Double-caped-ghosted
Around a burning cross
Sexothon psychosis ritual
Castrates their inner image
Their ethic crimes
Mutilation of genital parts
Into bituminous God
White hoods disclose how black
The manacled mind mutation
Issue forth Sulphanilic acid

Chronos, O Chronos!

Ethos anchored
Measured, plantation dominion
Infibulated guilt
The crossed teeth of dragon's foam
Democracy!

Said
Be still century

Down from Virginia to Carolina
Through Georgia to Alabama
Disperse west towards Mississippi
Arkansas
Up from Texas to Missouri
Kansas and Nebraska
Blood
       Lineage
             Legend

White heads of senile Negroes
Swaying in the southern air
Like fields of cotton

Color of skin erosion
South of bone intrusion
Atavistic inbred incestuous
Dynasty
Lost found Eldorado

Of the New World

Chronos, O Chronos!

Vector of V-bone population
Drunk on blood of my fathers
    Drunk on blood of my sons

                    Drunk on blood of my daughters
                        Drunk on wine of my husbands
                Chromosome plasmic virginal

Said to my eye sockets

                Chose between change
                And change, between choice
                And static noise
                Fire and water
                Chose

Said to my bones

                Century metaphored
                Time
                Masquerades on flesh
                Race of people hollowed out
                Meta-plexity solar miosis
                Come forth energy of violets
                Fire forever
                Steel and alloy
                By anvil and scopine
                Dialectic
                        Calamine
                            Asbestos
                Rhetoric of soil and water

And I said to my bones
Do you understand these violets
Ringing in the shingles of this house

                    Between chaos and chaos
                        Between peace and chaos
                            Between chaos and time
                                Between noise and solitude
                                Between chaos and life

            Between air, motion, stability
              Continuity and eternity

There is change

Effluvium of civilizations
Refracted   reflections

Hands
Corroded
In history
Prenatal, ageless foam
The mainland shores
Democracy!

Elemental soil
Elemental century

Images clear as nothing
Marble mellow faces distorted

Said

Axe and axe
The
Wheels
Turn
They grind inaudibly
    They grind inevitably
All metamorphizes
Cults fall, institutions, traditions
Orthodoxies   decay
Axe and axe
The
Wheels
Grind

Eternity stays not enough
Lightyears
To   stand still
The wind tears space through
Steel, etherizing revolution
Materializing power
Is suffering to grow —
Give us God, Oh

Give us water and fire!

Before wind nestled in robin's throat
  Before robin's throat
    Before wheel or steamship
      Before utterance, water, hieroglyphics
        Consonant or vowel
Before law before flint
Before chaos before light
  Before darkness walked naked from
    Her cave
      Prior to birth prior to death
        Prior to nothing
There was change

And I heard my soul singing

Presence necessitates absence
Everything inherently produces
Its non-thing
Its crisis
Existence is sustained
Is preserved away by counter-existence
Which is change, which
Is time
Wherefore in the absence and presence
Of place and non-place

Time and change render permanence possible
And impossible

Soul
Do you understand these violets

    Bone-rayed against rigor mortis
    Stone on stone rage
    We are fathomed out
        We are
        Blade to canyon
            Neptune to mountain
                To flint
    To these voices singing
    In the limbs of this house
    Nostalgia of heroic memory
    Oh, terrible choruses!

Singing in the soul

    Bee-wax, ghost of afterbirth
    And other fleeing furniture
    Upon that lonesome hill
    Climb down
        Descend
            Descend
    Into that mysterious onslaught
    Preserve ... preserve ...
    Oh rage!

    Through a burning glass
    Time consumes
    Between socket of eye
    Element, soil, pillows of granite
    Is strength in decision
    Chose to pass

Visions strutting upon that
Water   come down

And I heard my soul

Whispering
The one who rides in middle
Of the wind
Is thrashing this house
To eternity, listen
          Listen

Upon gothic doors
Fierce knuckles sound
The coming of Chronos
Our bones shake and tremble
  Our bones fragile and coward
      Dim the oil
        Hang static from our corners
Like dead foliage

Elemental
Centennial
In geode

Syndromes explode ethos
And the clocks cry out
Ontological dream
  House of Nightsong
    Legend
      Heritage
        Lineage
In our relentless fall
And climb
Give us God, oh

Give us water and fire!

Water and fire!

Part Three: Time for a Change

I

One hundred years the world has leaked into my bones
This land and this house have brought forth the traffic of
       my labour like ancient rivers bringing ships to harbor
       season after season
And, like the rivers, this land and this house have reclaimed
       all that was yielded up
And, in time, they themselves shall be taken away
I no less shall be reclaimed

At last I know this now

Living and dying are names for change
This house is a form in and through which time exercises change
To exist is to experience perpetual change
Time is change
The soul is time
The soul is a rock in motion
Living and dying are names for the same rock

II

How still the limbs and blood vessels of this house
How ghostly the staircase, how laden with dust the closets
How empty the many rooms

What is the soul
Who knows the soul when it walks up to meet you and shakes your hand
Folks say your background is your soul

They say still water runs deep
They say blood is thicker and more adhesive than tallow
Folks says this and folks say that

People say institutions will go on the same
People say law and traditions will go on the same
The South will go on walking in the usual stride by the Mississippi
        at the usual hour every sunset
Georgia will remain Georgia
The ways of southern folks change, if at all, gradually,
        imperceptibly, and neither law or force of arms can
        interdict the Allmighty will of God
People say
People say this and people say that

III

The news
Look at what passes for news nowadays
You will not find the news in history books, old magazines
        or current newspapers
I have seen a hundred years of news
Twelve sons and seven daughters have walked out of my womb
        to live in this house and then to pass from it
        into the world out yonder
Three husbands and God knows how many lovers have taken
        my body for healing
I have seen populations come and populations go, have had
        seven sons killed in five wars, have buried grandchildren
        and all my sisters, and seen rich fields full of burnt
        stumps while starving children ate their own flesh
I know about the news

Even now, here in the twenty-seventh corner of this house
        I can feel the news crumbling beneath my feet and
        around my body
Look into my face the news is etched and eroded

I see iron monsters coming up the hillside to this community,
        clawing and defacing, wrecking and rebuilding

I see people moving off this land, oozing into the teeming
          cities like Atlanta and Birmingham where they will be
          strangers and many will die
I see factories rising up, I see smoke stacks, I see new men
          and women, strangely tongued, New Englanders, Yankees,
          Westerners
I see negras, hooded heads throned with the crown of their
          new liberties, pretending they are not afraid of their
          new slavery
I see money-lenders, whore-masters and whores,
I see strife, violence, conflict and mongrelization of the races,
          white women will soon have black babies, and not just
          the other way around
I see the bull frog pacing up and down the Mississippi, hands
          clasped behind his back, like a worried general contemplating
          a battle he will surely lose
I see a terrible, complicated freedom let loose among my people —

They say *industrialization*, they say *progress*, they say
          civilization
Folks say one thing
Folks say another thing
Folks say

IV

No longer does the mysterious scarecrow from the field come
          to knock upon my door at midnight
No more do the pigeons roost in my hair and the crevices of
          my ears
They and the scarecrow from the field, have abandoned this house,
          abandoned this land
Like the other fleeing furniture that have been swallowed up
          by the city, they sit now in Woolworth and Kress and
          munch their meals —

They say, they say
People say a whole lot of things

V

What is it to be a woman
There are things about being woman the world of men will
            never fathom
We are loved and we are hated
We are envied and we are loathed
Angels and stickriders —
In the ultimate thrust of truth, every woman born slips to
            become a part of her own birth
My bones tell me the news is more than I am willing to accept
My hair has grown throughout this house and hangs down over the
            cracking stone like weeping moss
For I have been here alone so long searching for my children
            and my husbands and for the hands of the field

People say a house grows cold when love and hate pass out of it
People come out here from Atlanta saying my baby, Bobbie, died
            fifteen years ago in a war in a place called Iwo Jima
They say a house rots down when you live in one of its rooms
            for over fifteen years
They say the voices I hear are rodents and crocodiles and lizards
            who have taken over every ligament and bone fibre of this
            great house, except the twenty-seventh corner where I am
They say the mysterious scarecrow from the field has bolted
            all entrances and exits to this house
            and the pigeons are waiting for me down there where the
            sun rolls around on the ground like a crazy ball
And they say I have one of their machines up here that brings
            me the news from the fartherest corners of the world
            out yonder
Who goes upon that lonesome hill

Who is she who tears the husk from the corn and feeds the
        fowls of the air
Who is she who tames the furies of the hurricane and weep them
        for tears in lonely hours
The wind blew breath into Eve
And from her thighs she forked out Adam

VI

Here, in this house, custom and order will go on
Lactation has ceased but she, in the wind, who shakes these
        shingles and sinews away, will go on
Georgia will go on and Georgia will change
The South will go on and the South will change
The country and the world will go on and the country and
        the world will change
Men and women will be murdered and slaughtered, and men and
        women will be born and nurtured
The double-dying of she who rides in the middle of the wind
        will reign in the world like an idiot fire
And every woman sees in whichever man she gives her sex the
        potentiality of her whorehood

People say, People say

The confident woman as well as those afflicted in the abdomen
        and sphincter muscles
I recall long ago I slept with many men, even with one of the
        bucks of the field
I masturbated by finger and other bric-a-brac
I dreamed of great distorted phalluses rising up like cobras to
        lure me away to the unexplained canyons
I recall I often slept naked
Both accidental and by deliberate seizure, I have stroked and
        caressed my breasts and womb until sighs of awful release
        oozed from my constricted throat

And the dream, the nightmare:
Night after night I was somewhere in a dark cave with no exit
It was never clear how I got there
It always started with me just *there* in the dark cave, naked
        and surrounded by a hundred black negras.
At first I always thought they wanted to rape me one by one
            but then it would dawn on me that the black bucks were
                making fun of me, were dancing around and mocking my body —
                and I would discover why
It seemed my hands were webbed to the flesh of my vagina, and
            I had been born that way and it was horrible,
                and I would start crying and trying to free my hands
                and the wild laughter of the negras and their free swinging
                genitals would drive me insane
And then — it always happened:
Somehow, in great pain and agony, I would tear my hands free
            blood and bits of flesh would be all over the cave,
Instantly the dark cave would become illuminated in a magnitude
            which only the flames of hell could equal
A strange thing always happened — I would look up and around,
            and all of those black negra faces were white as snow!

Living and dying are two halves of the same stone
People say your background is your heritage
And that cats and horses and other animals can see ghosts and
        spirits

VII

One hundred years is time enough to come face to face with
        the soul
Below I see men working
They are big men with big machinery, and wear their shirts off
            some of them are black and their huge muscles glisten
            in the summer sun

I see them with bull-dozer and crane and wrecking hearse,
        working, digging, slowly but irrepressibly working their
        way to this house
I see how the sweat rolls down the contour of their flesh
        see how their trousers cling to their hips and sag
        in front as from some delicate heaviness inside
        see them gulp down water with an animal urgency
        that frightens me and yet somehow fascinates me —
And I know music is not what makes song universal
I know it is the quality of loneliness, it is the quality of
        suffering and the relentless passion to keep on living
        and loving and hating that make sound in any language
        speak to everyman

VIII

The news has come into my sightless eyes like grains of pepper
        blows through networks of fish entrails strung on poles
        all over the world out yonder

It is the mystery in our sex
The power of this mystery that gives a woman's body tenderness
        to render a grown man helpless and contented upon her
        breast like a baby
I remember when there were eyes in my thighs, when there were
        daisies in my tongue
My ears were wombs, the dimple in my right cheek was a scintillating
        womb
When I bent my arms and curled my limbs the calves and folds
        of my flesh were wombs
Between my toes and fingers were wombs
My mouth was a great womb
And there were one million un-named mysteries in the delicatessen
        of my flesh

Through the years I learned how to handle men
I wore oil skin, bathed in swamp water, pissed the juice of fish
Ate many fine vegetables
I knew how to extract the mother-wish from the coldest and
        hardest of men
Knew how to make men lust after my body and my spirit in which
        the medicine of my body was contained

People say, People say

But, even then, as now, I was lonely
People say no beautiful woman need be lonely
But few men can seldom be taught to lust after the God in a woman

Loneliness is the inherent hunger of being a damn good woman

IX

The news
You have asked me repeatedly about the news
What enigma haunts this house

From my hair and ears the pigeons have gone to the city and
        taken up residence in furnished rooms with various people who
        earn their money by gambling and playing bit parts in
        movies
My Bobbie is dead and I never told him the truth

Being white sometimes shields the truth away from us
The resemblance of truth, however, will haunt us and play
        fierce nightmares in our dreams
Being black will sometimes separate the truth from us

Oh Lord, now that the hour is at hand, to whom shall we turn!

There are those who march around in circles with placards
        protesting
There are those who gladly go to jail resisting, advancing
There are those all over the world out yonder marching, marching,
        the cancer of war ticking under the breast, the cancer
        of peace festering in the brain
From there is given to nations and races no property which is
        more than fabricated goodwill!
And the news does not come into the eyes
The news comes out of the eyes!

X

Alas! — let this house come down
Tradition, law, ethos, order, peace, morality
Nation after nation, race upon race, tribes, cliques, factions,
        movements, religions, cult and occult
Let them walk up to the soul stripped naked and recognize it
        in a test tube of sin and madness

What avail is it what people say
We are going to suffer now
I do not protest the expensive manufacturing of suffering
Why should I protest
I want to see more taxes levied for the appropriation of suffering
Let the iron-winged rodents spray this universe with the pungent
        fragrance of ever more and more scientific cancer
Oh what a stupendous spectacle it will be to see millions and
        millions of children born with eyeballs missing,
        walking around, and an arm or finger suddenly drops off,
        and little boys with their penises eaten away
        little girls with both hands webbed to their sex!

Yes, you men out there with the wrecking crew! —
Come! —
Let's get on with your business!

XI

Who goes upon that lonesome hill again and again? —

Death will come long, too long

In cancer the unfit will not survive
In cancer the fit will not survive
In this last hour of my century turning, I will not go out like
        so much box-wood, rag-mop, or white trash
In dignity I will stand here and defend this house to the end
I will fight, like all men and women, for what possesses my
        will
And it has nothing to do with right or wrong or good or evil
It has to do with God who is the essence of right and wrong
        and good and bad
        and yet who is beyond both right and wrong, both good and
        evil

I, Eleanor Nightsong, am Great!
Sweet loving and elemental
Am One with God

God is *change*

God is Chronos!

Medicine Man

from "LES DEUX MEGOTS MON AMOUR" (1985)

I had my own style, and I had my own realm of symbolism. I certainly had my own content, my own material, which was social in nature, and yet extremely personal as well [. . .] [I] was a long form poet. We all write short ones every now and then, what David Henderson called, "left hand hooks." But our main menu consists of long poems, poems you can get around inside of, sit down in, lie down in, walk and sleep and wake up in, make love in, and figure out what life is about in.

Medicine Man

North of Dark
North from Shango
In kangaroo jungle of West Lost
Dressed in hide of fox
Dressed at last to kill
Thirteen grains of sand
Seven memories
And Ten voices whispering in a rock

Time medicine riddle
Time rock disguised in evil bite
In devil flight
Time encloses cycles
Voice memory
Revolve
Age leaps upon the lips
Hawk! Kiss of hatred
Is turtle blood
Is love's hair buried in an old tin can

Then I said to my knee bones
Teach me how to bend
My knee bones hardening seven memories
Recalled what I fail to know
In an estranged familiar tongue
Said:
      If you must go
      Go by the abandoned railroad yard

The muddy ditch
The lizard infested by-pass
Flank to the left where an old black woman

With prayers for you in her wrinkled hands
Cupped in an old-fashioned apron lap
Rocks eternally
Eternal rock
Rocking chair
Pause, leave a tear
Beneath the fallen viaduct
But do not linger
For the road back is never
Home is never where you were born

Oh Grandmother, figurine gris gris Goddess
Do I
Should I
Can I live so that I may die easily

Thirty years wrinkle
My belly folds
When I sit
When I stand
My belly spreads

Thirty red years contending with Satan
The backbones breaking pain
Thirty times ten removed from gods
My fathers knew

Oh, Shango, man of mothers
Will you join us in trance
In eating of the bowels of black man
Who is our victim
Who no longer is father of his man

And do I approve
If I do not approve
I have done somebody wrong

If I do approve
Why should I approve
Thirty times ten removed from voices
Ancestral

Birth is April fish belly.
Love is love going the wrong way.
And if I weep
I weep for my twin rising out of
The marriage womb leaping upon me mid-years

Hence I put away old handed-down ailments
Put away hence common motives that drive men
To conventional madness
And weep for the mother of my twin
And conjure Dance on pages of medicine book
    of white hands
And by ceaseless slapping on genital organ
And by eating of embryo taken from ovaries
    of the dead infant boy
Leaping to meet me death
If I weep at all

We may not live until love
Until moon
And if I approve
Eating entrails of multitude of living victims
It will not resurrect those already dead
It will not heal ear and tongue of betrayal
April is a time of betrayal
And I do not approve
I do not approve

And if I pray
I pray not to God nor Shango
I pray to bellies of deep sea sharks

And pray for us survived west lost
North of dark in chains

After the present pain is gone.
The hate who roars in the brain.
The one who sucks my breath like an evil cigarette
The one who crushes the young men and smashes them
Who will be left to care

So shameless black men speak blood of their sisters!
And will it if I weep
Drive away juju of the fox
And if I pray
I have done somebody wrong

And if I do not pray
I pray for those who will live until moon
And to those residing in evil bite
And to the old black woman living in my wounds
And for the twin of the father who falters

I pray because I was born
And have sinned my birth to clay.

Wherefore I said to my knee bones
Instruct me how to stand
Teach me how to love and how to die
And my bones wherein the hot oil
Of the sun is contained
Said:
        Go by the abandoned railroad yard
        Flank to the left your black mamma
        Is rocking
        Seven memories recall what
        You know
        North of the dark path in juju jungle

Age leaps upon the lips and caresses
The kiss of wisdom is love
Hold thirteen grains of sand
Look at the sun until it three-times
Blinds you, and listen
Listen to ten voices
Singing in that rocking chair

Singing in that rock!
Singing in that rock!

✳   ✳   ✳

Almost Sunday

From Gany Mede to cat of mountain
I have borne the sentient seasons
At best
Burning down tenement buildings
Martin Luther King eater of the flame.

At anvil trembling
On this earth
Strung-out between station and no station
Between tarrying and fleeing
I am naked and shiver in fear
Serpent spears glint the night
Teeth of those who eat my back
Mock the face of Taurus.

If I were your poet, America!
Who walk in sun or dusklight
With black mothers of children
Betwixt eyes of white, blue
And hectic green,
Injecting easter eggs with blood

Of the assassinated fathers,
Bareboned striding footways
Of Fred Douglass —
You would hound me down, say I was
A mentally deranged Negro gone mad
Under stress of the civilized weight.

Starting from Tennessee, from Lookout
Mountain,
Heeding the hurt to sing,
Up the coast East or West
Now the wars lock.

I, Child of Wolf, paws marred
In marred lore of the Gift Outraged,
Stalk your streets of prey;

And in every painted face
Brace my skin for the grin of Janus,
Trans-substantiate my iniquity
To song
And almost Sabbath.

*   *   *

Taurus by Aster Fire

To Ree Dragonette

I

Moon and sun
By fire alone we blend.

Aster is the moon
Taurus is the sun
April is the fire
And the second sign leaks blood down the zodiac

Who then is prepared to travel rays
Of sun to where sun is?

When the eternal broomrider hammer python teeth
Into hip and thyroid
When the middle period leaps upon the breath
Debris accrete in the eyeball
And the salivating organs recoil like leaves
That are withered
Who is going to love us then?

II

Who are the young women dressed in variegated orange
Who are the bagpipes that steal upon our graves
And who walks rays of blood
To where moon is?

III

Love is a difficult medicine.

Say *toro*
Whose hide is pagan saint
Harassed by the jewels of the firmament
Centered in the ring, the matador's
Scorpion biting his primitive cranium,
He beats and paws the earth down.
The matador is streak of lightning solidified
The matador is dance without motion
Is bone lean in hectic orange.

From bull to matador the link
In blood and steel
Is forged —
From Africa to the West by aster moon

Grotesque vessels stalk the seas —
Tartar . . . Jesus . . . Amistad . . .
Triangular cargo triangular trade
Rum paste flesh sugar spice cocoa
New England gentleman, Spanish captain,
Virginia aristocrat, Italian driver,
Mandingo wench, Ashanti buck.

Now the charge
The elemental
Beast and man, man and beast
The instigating multitudes drive them blind
In the invisible floodlights of insanity
Blood of both streak the sky
Olé!

IV

Are we dead
Are we dead
Everywhere are we dead to the madness of dying?

Affirm dragon angel
Wooly and snarling, heave into her fire
And mate
Oh what have you done with your muleta
Oh why were there a sword behind your muleta
Say *toro*!

V

Orange is April *banderilla.*

We have enjoyed and abused one another
We need other people to love and to hate
We need other people to mark occasion and

Shield away as well as consummate flesh,
Life and death and marriage and birth —
As organism recedes into decay
We will be loved by those who come at
Perennial
Old hates will be rekindled
Old loves will be rekindled
New Love and new hate will be born:
Who are sons and daughters and grandsons
And granddaughters gathered on occasion
Who are cousins, in-laws, and who on what
Branch of constellation
Who rides Sagittarius, Who has
Scorpio's nose
Clarissa wedded a Jew
George could not get in from sea
Who dead, who gotten old
Who do not look a day older than
The last time who gathered here
And whose photographs are yellowing but who
Bring back memory
Come, we must put down more names in the
Book of numbers and take more photographs
For the book of seasons.

The dead go on living
The living go on dying
Generation generation generation
We do not die and we die.

VI

The physical world whirls in its orbit
The spiritual world whirls in its orbit
The orbits of the physical and the spiritual
Are integral whirls.

In the turning of the zodiac
Pole to pole
Umbra to umbra
In the turning
Who will traverse aster rays to where
Constellations bleed!

Forever wedded
Forever torn
Sun and Moon
By fire we blend.

*   *   *

A Ballad of the Life and Times of Joe Louis, The Great Brown Bomber

I

Know I must and think I will
Sound the gong and make a song of shimmering steel
And make it real
For the Great Brown Bomber born on the Buckalew Mountains
    among the Alabama Hills!

Lesser men
    who raving
    who babble senility
    who name lakes after themselves who eyes glint
    who lips twitch
Are not abandon to shipwreck cold and naked shock
    but are
    paraded before the world
    and live in mansions
If not in peace.

So come and go
Ye throngs of thousands, ye mermaids of cognition
Hail! Hail! Hail!
Come and go back to fireside chats and the gospel songs
    of the Golden Gate Quartet,
Come and go
    when I was a boy down in Chattanooga Tennessee
    when black folks congregate in Big Mable's bootlegged
    liquor joint
    and children hovered outside against the storefront
    windows painted black all the way up to the heights of our
    wool-laden heads
    when the entire ghetto street grew quiet
    in open daylight
    when pride quelled beating hearts still
    and over the only wireless in the neighborhood
    we stood as though around a throne
And all ears awaited the sound of the gong.

II

Hail! Hail! Hail!
        JUNE 22nd 1938
         YANKEE STADIUM
          ROUND ONE
    LOUIS COMES OUT MAKING A WINDING MOTION WITH HIS RIGHT
    FOREARM
Just like the first time
    AND HE SENDS A RIGHT TO SCHMELING'S JAW THAT STAGGERS
    THE BIG GERMAN
    NOW LOUIS SENDS ANOTHER, A THIRD, A FOURTH, ALL HITTERS!
And unlike the first time
    LOUIS DOES NOT DROP HIS GUARD AFTER HITTING THE GERMAN
    UNLIKE THE FIRST TIME
    NOW SCHMELING TRIES TO COUNTER WITH A FUSILLADE OF RIPPING
    RIGHTS AND LEFTS

BUT JOE JERKS BACK
SCHMELING BORES IN AND TOUCHES A LIGHT ONE LOUIS IGNORES IT
NOW THEN BUT LOUIS SMASHES HOME A RIGHT THAT SHOULD
HAVE DENTED CONCRETE DENTED CONCRETE DENTED CONCRETE!!!

And the nation exploded: "Beat That German. Brown Bomber,
    Beat That German!"
As if to himself the crippled man in the White House in the fireside
    chair murmured: "Beat The Nazi, Beat Him For The Morale Of
    The American Democracy!"
And in big Mabel's bootlegged liquor joint up and down the street
    everywhere shouted to the sky: "Whop Him, Joe, Baby, Whop
    Him For The Sake Of Colored Folks All Over Dhis Forsaken Land!"

WHEELING SCHMELING FACE FRONT TO THE ROPES JOE LOUIS SENDS
A VICIOUS RIGHT TO THE KIDNEY
Why does the announcer call Joe's punch "Vicious"?
Were it the other way around . . .
A VICIOUS RIGHT TO THE KIDNEY VICIOUS TO THE KIDNEY AND
SCHMELING SCREAMS LADIES AND GENTLEMEN
SCREAMS IN PAIN PAIN PAIN WHEELING SCHMELING FACE FRONT
TO THE ROPES OH MY COUNTRY ROPES OF THEE BLACK NECKS HANGING
FROM THE POPLAR TREES MY COUNTRY TEARS OH VICIOUS RIGHT
TO THE KIDNEY AND THE GERMAN BLOND SCREAMS IN AGONY
ONE OF THE MOST TERRIFYING SOUNDS HEARD IN THE RING
LADIES AND GENTLEMEN
In the first round of the first fight when the Brown Bomber entered
    the ring and took off his robe
    there was another scream sounded the same
    hysterical scream from a WOMAN at ringside:
EEEEEEEEEEOOOOOOOOOOOOOOOOOOOOOOO–WWWWWWWWWW!!!!!!
WHATS THAT HE GOT IN HIS PANTS OH GOD WHATS THAT RIG BULGING
IN HIS JOCKSTRAP

The Most Terrifying Sound Ever Heard In The Ring!

MAX SCHMELING STRUGGLES TO LIFT HIS RIGHT ARM TO GRAB
THE SIDE THE RIB THE GOOD OLD BAR B QUED RIB BUT MAX IS
PARALYZED PARALYZED
REFEREE ARTHUR DONOVAN STEPS BETWEEN LOUIS AND THE GERMAN
AND THE BROWN BOMBER IS POISING ANOTHER BOMB

Get Away, Joe! screams Referee Donovan

LOUIS BLINKS AND BACKS AWAY GLARING ANGRILY AT THE WRITHING
GERMAN . . . *scenes of flashing back images montage what a ball*
of cotton with a great dictator mustache walking arrogantly
from the olympic stands vowing he'd never recognize no black
coon even if he were the fastest man alive! . . . PEOPLE YELL FOR
THE COUNT START THE COUNT THE COUNT BUT NO COUNT BEGINS
MAX IS UTTERLY HELPLESS AND BUT FOR THE ROPES HE WOULD BE
FLOPPED ALREADY HIS BLOND HEAD IS ROLLING LIKE RUBBER
NOW THEN LOUIS HITS HIM WITH A SWISHING HOOK WITH A RIFLE
TWIST TO IT SCHMELING DROPS BUT BEHOLD STAGGERS UP ON KNOCKING
KNEES WITHOUT TAKING A SINGLE COUNT WOO WOO WOO THE GERMAN
MUST REALLY BE SUPERMAN
NOW THEN BUT LOUIS AGAIN FLOORS THE GERM . . . SOMETHING WHITE
AN ILLEGAL TOWEL HAS BEEN THROWN INTO THE RING FROM SCHMELING'S
CORNER THE REFEREE IS THROWING THE TOWEL BACK OUT OF THE
RING . . . BUT SCHMELING HAS CRUMPLED . . . FOR KEEPS . . .
REFEREE DONOVAN BREASTROKES WITH BOTH ARMS AND THE MASSACRE
IS ENDED WHERE SCHMELING WAKES UP IN THE HOSPITAL

Down in Chattanooga, Tennessee black men and women and children sang
    and wept and danced and prayed and rejoiced
And my grandmother said: "Lawd, childe, aint neber seed black folks
    be so proud, naw, not eben when ole Abraham Lincoln freed us
    aint neber seed black folks so hopeful, naw, not even when ole
Abe promised forty acres and one mule."
Hail! Hail! Oh, Hail!

III

I know I'm right and can't be wrong
Come along children and sing this song
And let it live
For the Great Brown Bomber born on the Buckalew Mountains
    among the Alabama Hills.

A pot of lye will sting and a bullet will kill
"Maw, I glad I win, I glad I win," quot the heavyweight champeen
O come along while the moon is shining bright
Gie me a pig feet and a bottle of gin
We gon raise the ruckus tonight!

IN EVERY MAIN BATTLE NO PERSON WHATEVER SHALL BE UPON THE
STAGE EXCEPT THE PRINCIPALS AND THEIR SECONDS: THE SAME RULE
TO BE OBSERVED IN THE BY-BATTLES, EXCEPT THAT IN THE LATTER
MR. BROUGHTON IS ALLOWED TO BE UPON THE STAGE TO KEEP DECORUM
AND TO ASSIST GENTLEMEN IN GETTING TO THEIR PLACES THESE ARE
MR. BROUGHTON'S RULES 1743

Fifty-nine heavyweight champeen fights fifty-one by knockout!
Flat feet stalker! Yo mamma wusnt no Mississippi delta queen
1619 nineteen Africans rattled their chains on the shores of
    Jamestown Virginia didnt come to America on no flower of
    May secking no dream for

The white dream is a black nightmare.

ON THE MEN BEING STRIPPED IT SHALL BE THE DUTY OF THE SECONDS
TO EXAMINE THEIR DRAWERS, AND IF ANY OBJECTION ARISES AS TO
THE INSERTION OF IMPROPER SUBSTANCES THEREIN THEY SHALL APPEAL
TO THEIR UMPIRES WHO WITH THE CONCURRENCE OF THE REFEREE SHALL
DIRECT WHAT ALTERATIONS SHALL BE MADE THESE ARE LONDON PRIZE
RING RULES 1838 REVISITED 1853
And a white woman screamed at ringside . . . *Here are the fruits for the*
    wind to suck and the buzzards to pluck

seeds often thousand black men dripping blood
from the magnolia tree . . .
STOPPING A FIGHT A MOMENT TOO SOON MAY BE UNFAIR TO
A GAME MAN: STOPPING IT A MOMENT TOO LATE MAY BE A TRAGEDY
SO SAITH ARTHUR DONOVAN
Runt fat men hallucinating jungle hunters, playing tough guys
Writing novels of wild life and statuesque imperialists
  with shotguns in their mouths
Jack London switching alongside the stout black legs of Jack Johnson
Burnt-out Hebrew novelist jerking off his dukes at the bicep pistons
  of the baddest black man ever to leap out of the criminology books
Who fought his way from nothing and nobody to the Heavyweight
  Champeenhood of the known world, alas, to be
Found "mysteriously" dead for seven nights and seven days

Oh Hail! Hail! Hail!
Jersey Joe Sugar Ray Floyd Patterson Kid Gavaland Archie Moore
Gentleman Jim John G. Chamber and the Marquis of Queensberry —
Oh, Hail to the Contest of Endurance!

IV

Maybe I'm wrong and don't care if 1 am
But I believe I will
Sound the gong *Flam Flam Flam*
For the Great Brown Bomber who rose above the Buckalew Mountains
  and the hills of Alabam.

BORN: 1914 May 13th TAURUS:
First decanate: Sub-ruler, Venus
Constellation: LEPUS
Of African Indian and Caucasian blood
Making money making money making money FOR WHOM

The gong tolls?

MARVA! Fine brownskin middle-class fashion-struck woman prancing
   through celluloid cities of Paris, London, Madrid

Hanging out with Josephine Baker
   scream of a woman at ringside . . .

Jockstrap of the Bull!

Stalking Jabbing Stalking Jabbing Stalking Chunking bomb after bomb
   after bomb into the bodies of other men
   fighting as many as eight fights a year!

1937 Chicago Knock out James J. Braddock

1937 New York defeated Tommy Farr

1938 New York Knock out Nathan Mann

1938 New York Knock out Harry Thomas

1938 New York Knock out Max Schmeling

1939 New York Knock out John H. Lewis

1939 Los Angeles Knock out Jack Roper

1938 New York Knock out Tony Galento

1939 Detroit Knock out Bob Paster

1940 New York defeated Arturo Godey

1940 New York Knock out Johnny Paycheck

1940 New York Knock out Arturo Godey

1940 Boston Joe Louis Knocked out Al McCoy

1941 New York Joe Louis Knocked out Red Berman

1941 Philadelphia Joe Louis Knocked out Gus Derazio

1941 Detroit Joe Louis Knocked out Abe Simon

1941 St. Louis Joe Louis Knocked out Tony Muste

1941 Washington D. C. Joe Louis whipped Buddy Baer

1941 New York Joe Louis Knocked out Billy Conn

1941 New York Joe Louis Knock out Lou Nova

1942 New York Joe Louis Knock out Buddy Baer

1942 New York Joe Louis Knock out Abe Simon

And then
   around the world

BROOM ... BROOM ... BRRRRROOOOOOOOMMMMMMMMMMM
                    PEARL HARBOR!
            UNCLE SAM WANTS YOU   boy
Uncle Sam God Damn Hush!   yo mouf
            SLIP OF THE LIP MIGHT SINK A SHIP
            TODAY EUROPE TOMORROW THE WORLD
Exhibition fights for Uncle Sam's morale
But do not go near the white frenchy women, boy
Or you'll find your neck swinging from the ropes
scream of a woman ...
            NOTHING TO FEAR BUT FEAR ITSELF
PATHE NEWS: Knockout Tojo: PATHE NEWS: all chickens cackle when
    the ROOSTER crows: One down Two to go
PATHE NEWS: Atomic Bomb!
Hey, boy, you may be the Brown Bomber but we got a Bomb that gonna
    knock out ten million chinks before you can throw a punch
Oh, Hail! Hail! Hail!
ATOMIC BOMB!

V

Stars and Stripes forever!
Five winters past
Stars and Stripes
Name a bottle of gin "Joe Louis"
    Spirit of Lightning
    The Knock Out Liquor
Five summertimes in the matador's ring,
Taurus possessor of healing powers divinely given
Whom shall you fight five winter ages gone, Olé!

            WEDNESDAY NIGHT JUNE 19th 1946,
                    YANKEE STADIUM
45, 266 SPECTATORS FAN THE WITNESS BOX
1, 925, 564 DOLLARS RESIDE AT THE BOX OFFICE

Give us pause: Arthur Donovan all time fight referee
                    Jo Humphreys all time fight announcer
    having died during the interim of the duration
Before the fight give them pause.

BILLY CONN FOOT FLEET NIMBLE FOR EIGHT ROUNDS
BACKING AWAY DANCING SIDE TO SIDE BACKPEDDLING BICYCLING
NEW REFEREE EDDIE JOSEPH AS WELL AS THE NEW ANNOUNCER ARE
OUT OF BREATH TRYING TO KEEP APACE WITH THE SKATING BUTTERFLY
OF THE RING LADIES AND GENTLEMEN
BUT NOW EARLY IN THIS ROUND BILLY AINT MOVING FAST ENOUGH
AND JOE CATCHES HIM WITH A WICKED LEFT HOOK AND A SHARP
TEARING RIGHT HANDER

                "He Can Run But He Can't Hide"

THE SECOND PUNCH, THE SHARP, TEARING RIGHT HANDER, RIPPED
OPEN A GASH UNDER THE BUTTERFLY'S LEFT EYE AND BILLY IS HURT
BUT NOT IN REAL TROUBLE NOT YET
NEVERTHELESS CONN'S LEGS DO NOT CARRY HIM BACKWARDS WITH THE
SAME EARLIER SPEED AND JOE IS ON TOP OF HIM ON TOP OF HIM
AND LOUIS HITS CONN FIVE FIVE FIVE FIVE FIVE PUNCHES IN
A BLISTERING FUSILLADE ALL IN THE SPACE OF SECONDS
AND ALL TO THE HEAD . . .

[*Hey, Joe! Joe of Louis, why don't you come and go with me*
Back down to Chattanooga Tennessee
I aint got a dime and I dont own a buffalo
But you and me Joe we are Tauruses We got hearts full of magnolias
    and lilacs and green grass in our loins
Face it everybody loves a winner but when you lose you lose alone
And it is cold out here among the pale stone
Please Joe
Come with me, do not let them drive you too like the rest
    into those anonymous ruins where
    haggard nurses stalk the silence

And forgotten men sit idle exhuming wisdom in
Oblivion's concern]

...ALL TO THE HEAD
THE LAST ONE IS A MURDEROUS RIGHT CROSS AND BILLY CONN SAGS
LOUIS FIRES A HARD LEFT THAT STAGGERS CONN, AND FOLLOWS WITH
A HARD LEFT AND RIGHT THAT STRETCHES CONN ON HIS BACK ON THE
FLOOR WHERE REFEREE JOSEPH COUNTS HIM OUT FULL "TEN" AT TWO
MINUTES NINETEEN SECONDS OF THE EIGHT AND FINAL ROUND
Final for Conn Final for Conn and Finally
An omen for you too Joe.

VI

So now we sit here in the year of nineteen hundred and seventy-one.
What happened to all that money you made
What happened to your fortune
Oh, Birds! Birds! Birds!
We stand idle inside of trembling fists
    where no gongs
Bat the ringing in our spines limp and old

Yes, Old!

When first I journeyed from Chattanooga seeking strange
    insistent voices
To New York, expecting to actually find you walking the streets
    of Harlem, strong and proud and hear you speak to me alone
    characteristically as Billie Holiday might have spoken
    had she escaped,
I was disappointed.
Not with you but with the world!
For you are not merely my hero of old but hero of all time
    for all black men and women whirlwinding within the
    gift outraged;

94

But your friends, your wives, the multitude of hangers-on
Where are they — are they with you now?

I am with you Joe Louis
I am with you in your strange surroundings and in your fears,
    for, unbeknowing to those who write copy and those who put
        on parties,
Your fears are *my* fears — Oh, God! How real they really are!

Hail! Hail! Hail!
I walked with you when you were up and in
I walk with you now although you are out you are not down
    and never will
Oh, Hail! Great Brown Bomber born on the Buckalew Mountains
    among the Alabama Hills!

＊　＊　＊

The Patient: Rockland County Sanitarium

For Portia

I

Here is a place that is no place
And here is no place that is a place
A place somewhere beyond time
And beyond the reaches of those who in time
Bring flowers and fruit to this place,
Yet here is a definite place,
And a definite time, fixed
In a timelessness of precise vantage
From which to view flowers and view fruit
And view those who come bearing them.

Those who come by Sunday's habit are weary
And kiss us half-foreign but sympathetic;

Spread, eat noisily to crack the unbearable
Silence of this place —
They do not know that something must always come
From something and that nothing must come always
From nothing, and that nothing is always a thing

To drive us mad.

II

A little at a time. Time is little,
Obsolescent and eternal.
Those who come Sundayly kiss us
And place flowers in our windows
While their minds grow smaller than the Eyes
Of the serpent who is at the gate:
Christ was not a man but a woman who wept for man.

Time is absolute, fluid, and infinite,
Origin and destiny, beginning and end,
Wedded and unwedded in the endless beginningless —
Faces that are distorted and terrified, faces
That are marble and mellow, all laugh the same
And weep the same both here and there.
Society is the hero.
Society is the villain.

Here, however, in Rockland Sanitarium, one can see them
Existentially;
Know, at last that neither exist!

III

But if I were to speak mouth fully
Eat it and grow fat like you, oh so
Fat — and lielays, of course, with discretion,

Laylies, and vagina centric like you,
I could not, with the help of God, distinguish
Trash from trash: the fragments of shattered lives
Hang in broken windows —
Throw them out!

I choose rather to speak confusedly with the
World that swirls around within and without the gate;
Trapped now here and trapped there everywhere
And nowhere in wellsfargoland, ambushed at the hour
Of birth and before and after, set upon by rats and roaches
Between definitional montanas, between left and left
And right and right and nothing and everything between
No place and some place without and within:
The whole world is our patient, dear ones.

IV

So it is best to keep silent
Ask no questions, give no answers, make no
Responses.
At least, this way, we let them that know us not;
The world knows us not, Portia;
For we are no longer dwellers in the world,
But, having once been a part of it and learned
Its awful truth, have passed beyond that terrible place.

Passed beyond struggle, beyond the motives that lead
To madness
Now to sit here resigned, dumb as dead soldiers are
And stare out upon the great hecatomb of life with cold,
Immobile, terrified eyes.

Scarecrow

Here the world is whistle of wind
Through stone-webbed ears
Where love hides the mind is stuffed
With old magazines and bones of spiders;
Here the eyes stare at black skies
From there is room, a room
Lie down cold in emptiness.

Here last scarecrow stalks narrow
Asphalt in search of bird, a hawk
That hawk, a shuck of corn flew
Nowhere from rain to lake
Of drown in sadness;
Here iron teeth grind up earth
Rock and magnolia; recall the boyhood wheel,
Wagon and horseshoe in the dirtdark
Under the house, phallus

> *Hi spy*
> *Bumba rye*
> *All my black birds hid!*

Here memories play truth primitive poetman
Grown lean and crooked down the profile
In echelons of pain
Dread and worry break on the heart
Like skeletons of rat's claw.

Where is she who once brought countryside
And milk to the lips of that scarecrow?
Rotten rag and dead cornsilk
Form there is death in sawdust and brittle semen
Where once bloomed chrysanthemum
And stately elephant ears.

Here and there a room has a million
Black thundering rods,
Is mazed with no sound
Sound or sleep at all
Except the dead noise of obsolete
Locomotives.

* * *

Fall Down

In memory of Eric Dolphy

All men are locked in their cells.
Though we quake
In fist of body
Keys rattle, set us free.

I remember and wonder why?
In fall, in summer; times
Will be no more. Journeys
End.
I remember and wonder why?

In the sacred labor of lung
Spine and groin,
You cease, fly away

To what? To Autumn, to
Winter, to brown leaves, to
Wind where no lark sings; yet
Through dominion of air, jaw and fire

I remember!

Eric Dolphy, you swung
A beautiful axe. You lived a clean

Life.
You were young —
You died.

* * *

D Blues

D blues
What you woke up wit
Dhis mourning
What you toss and turn
All night in your bed wit
Nothing, no
One in your arms
No
Body.

Dats
What D blues
Is.

Riots and Revolutions

from "DYNAMITE GROWING OUT OF
THEIR SKULLS!" (1968)

The spark that will set off the dynamite which is being cultivated within the Negro may well be the slightest incident, some little mishap, which, in the minds of most Americans, will have no connection with the explosion that shall ensue. But it will have a connection; it will be the boomerang, having gained momentum, returning to the source of its origin — the prodigal violence. Unlike most Americans, the existential Negroes are not blind to, or blinded by, reality; they have been grappling with the most horrible realities all of their lives. They know America from both inside and out, they are Americans and they are not Americans, they are possessors of double visions, double truths; they are not alienated from America, they are alienated within America; they are aware, more aware, of the presence of the Bomb than most white people are, and sense that annihilation haunts the entire human race; they discern the presence of violence in a society which has lost its community, its humanity — as when thirty human beings stand by as a woman is repeatedly attacked and finally murdered, or the assassination of the President, the murder of Medgar Evers, the maiming of those three young civil rights workers, and the killing of people in foreign lands (sometimes by accident and sometimes as if for sport). The existential Negroes know the meaning of these things, for they *are* the meaning of these things; their violence will not be their violence alone, their violence will be America's violence.

Terrorist

*For the four Negro children
murdered in Birmingham while
praying to God*

Like his strickened face
Stroke of midnight.
Torn by crack of thunder
Or dissonance of vowel,
The deed, like an agonized tooth
Fell from his mouth

And exploded.

In a dark room in a crumbling
Heart, the deed conceived its victims:
Ninety-one nails in the breast of Christ;
The deed made terror, ripped open

Flesh and bone. No one knew,
Not even he himself, eight fragile legs
Would never walk from that debris.
I am the door. Hammer me down

Ninety-one and four!
They were like chrysanthemums,
Tender flesh cracked by thunder —
Unknown to his grotesque face.

A revolution must draw blood.

In the manacled chamber of our egos
What we do not know about death

Comes alive; and though love agonized
There, when terror expires our frail hearts

Hate is a bitter madness.

For the four who died, without tears,
Outside of cognition — their end
Is everlasting;
Their beginning is eternity.

To die young, before the rodent of exchange
Imperils the flesh, when you are innocent
And immaculate to the paranoid itch,
Is lambs blood
Is bread trans-substantiated

To galaxy.

If I were loin from whose pain
The ecstasy of these four little girls
Leaped, I would wail and weep,

Seek revenge; fly, with shotgun,
Through the streets.
Yet, I know

When all this raving, tortured love
And flagellating hatred
Is reckoned up to stars,
These four will illuminate
The dark more than a billion heavens.

I wish I had died as they!
Before thunder in your face is
Done, you will too; there shall be

No shaking hands later on
And forgetting; blood will heave

In your chattered streets,
Birmingham!

And God, the tornado
Shall rave down on you like an angered
Black fist, merciless

And violent!
Unto the blazing sun.

* * *

The Mob

Summer sets on the cities like a hen
On a package with a ticking noise inside —
New York, Chicago, Birmingham,
Newark, Atlanta, Watts . . .

The sun is on fire.

We rise and go forth
Flesh withering, bones tinkling,
Tottering, we
Brace ourselves alone
Against stone
Protoplasm against steel
Rigid before the loneliness in
The other's skin.

Fire tongued to dead ears
Wintered selves
Digging graves in summertime.

There is something dreadful
About our being here this way, undulating
In the streets,
Blasted down, flesh scorched by liquid rays
Of baptismal hose,
Something abandoned, fetching
At the worm in the rock of our fists,
Something in the breast
Which the heart cannot
Or dare not utter.

When
If at last we meet
In death-threaded exigence
It is no accident we scream obscenity —
All our life is obscenity
There is nothing accidental about trash.

The sun also screams.

Ravished the sky, the junkyard,
The citied streets,
Forlorn we limp away:
Head helmets,
Body bayonets,
Bloody rags.

Jitterbugging in the Streets

To Ishmael Reed

There will be no Holy Savior crying out this year
No seer, no trumpeteer, no George Fox treading barefoot up and down
        the hot land
The only Messiah we shall see this year is a gunned-down man
          staggering to and fro
            through the wilderness of the screaming ghetto
Blotted out by soap opera housewives in the television afternoons
          exchanging gossip vomited up from cesspools
          of plastic lives
Talking to himself

An unshaven idiot!
A senile derelict!
Ugly black nigger!

Piety and scorn on the doormouth of the Lord
        instructing the populace to love thine oppressor, be kind to
        puppies and the Chaste Manhattan National Bank

Because of this there will be no Fourth-of-July this year
No shouting, no popping of firecrackers, no celebrating,
        no parade
But the rage of a hopeless people
Jitterbugging
      in
        the streets.

Jacksonville Florida Selma Alabama
Birmingham, Atlanta, Rochester, Detroit, Bedford Stuyvesant,
Jackson Mississippi Watts Los Angeles Harlem New York
Jitterbugging
      in
        the streets

To ten thousand rounds of ammunition
Water hoses, electrical prods, phallic sticks,
       hound dogs, black boots stomping in soft places
       of black bodies —
Venom on the tongues of Christian housewives,
       smart young Italians, old Scandinavians in Yorkville,
       businessmen, civil service employees, suntanned suburban
       organization men, clerks and construction workers, poor white
       folks and gunhappy policemen;

"WHY DON'T WE KILL ALL NIGGERS: NOT ONE OR TWO BUT EVERY DAMN
    BLACK OF THEM! NIGGERS WILL DO ANYTHING. I BETTER NEVER CATCH
    A NIGGER LOOKING AT MY DAUGHTER . . . AUGHTER GRAB EM UP AND SHIP
    EVERY BLACK OF THEM OUT OF THE COUNTRY . . . AUGHTER JUST LINE
    EM UP AND MOW EM DOWN MACHINEGUNFIRE!"

All Americans: loving their families, going to church regularly
    depositing money in their neighborhood bank
All Fourth-of-July celebrators vomited up from the guilt-ridden
    cockroach sick sex terror of the Eldorado of the West
Talking to themselves, fantasizing hatred
In drinking bars and public houses
On street corners and park benches
At bridge clubs and bingo games
And in fashionable midtown Manhattan restaurants.

Shame! Shame! Shame!

No Holy Savior shall cry out upon the Black Nation this year
No true believer, no trombonist, no coal train
The only Messiah black people will know this year is a bullet
In the belly
       of a black youth shot down by a coward crouched
       behind an outlaw's badge —
Mississippi
Georgia

Tennessee, Alabama
Your mother your father your brothers sisters
         wives sons daughters and loved ones
Up
And
Down
The hot land
                    There is a specter haunting America!
Spitfire of clubs, pistols, shotguns, and the missing
Murdered
Mutilated
Bodies of relatives and friends
Be the only Santa Claus black children will remember this year
Be the only Jesus Christ born this year curled out dead on the
         pavement, torso floating at the bottom of a lake.

You say there are twenty-five million blacks in America and one
         gate to the ghetto
Make their own bed hard and that is where they have got to lie
You say there is violence and lawlessness in the ghetto, niggers
         run amuck perpetrating crimes against property, looting stores,
         breaking windows, flinging beer bottles at officers of the law
You say a virgin gave birth to God
Through some mysterious process, some divine conjure, a messenger
         of the Lord turned his walking cane into a serpent, and the
         snake stood upright and walked away like a natural man
You say . . .

AMERICA, WHY ARE YOU SCARED OF THE SCARECROW?

I say!
There is TERROR in the ghettoes!
Terror that shakes the foundation of the very assholes
         of the people
And fear! And corruption! And Murder!

The ghettoes are the plantations of America
Rat infested tenements totter like shanty houses stacked upon
          one another
Circular plague of the welfare check brings vicious wine every
          semi-month, wretched babies twice a year, death and hopelessness
          every time the sun goes down
Big-bellied agents of absentee slumlords and trustee insurance
          companies and millionaire humanitarian philanthropists
Forcing little black girls to get down and do the dog before they
          learn how to spell their names — sleeping on the floor
They do not have beds to make hard!

He said he was fifteen years old
And as he walked beside us there in the littered fields of the
          Harlem Nation, he spoke with a dignity of the language that
          shocked us
And he said he had a *theory* about what *perpetrated* the horror
          that was upon us, walking among flying bullets, broken glass,
          curses and the ignorant phalluses of cops whirling about
          our bloody heads.
He said he was a business major at George Washington High School
And he picked up a bottle and hurled it above the undulating crowd
Straight into the chalk face of a black helmet! —
Thirty-seven Properties Ransacked
Steel Gates Ripped From Their Hinges
Front Panes Shattered
Pawn Shops   Dry Cleaners   Liquor Stores . . . Piggly Wigglies
Ripped
          apart
                    and
                         LOOTED!

"Niggers will do anything!"

And long as the sun rises in the East
Niggers, in dingy fish-n-chip and bar-b-q joints,

Will be doing business as usual —
From River to river,
Signboard to signboard
Dribbling Schaefer six-packs of beer all over the ghetto
Marques Haynes is a globetrotting basketball playing fool.

TERROR stalks the Black Nation
A Genocide so blatant
Black men and women die in the gutters as if they were reptiles
And every third child will do the dope addict nod in the whore-
   scented night before the fire this time
And Fourth-of-July comes with the blasting bullet in the mind
   of a black man
Against which no great white father, no social worker,
   no psychothanatopsis
Will nail ninety-nine *theses* to no door:
    Jitterbugging
      in
        the streets!

"Without a passport to humanity": London Poems

Now floating around in Europe, working on a novel (yet untitled), finding that only a handful of white men in the whole world are capable of ever treating a black man or woman as a human being. When I left America I was to the left of Martin Luther King; when I return, for I shall, and soon, I will be to the left of Malcolm X and Fanon.

* Hernton's contributor biography for *Black Fire: An Anthology of Afro-American Writing* (1968), edited by Amiri Baraka and Larry Neal

An Unexpurgated Communiqué to David Henderson

London — 1966

I

If you are qualified it is legal to be a dope addict in London
It is alright to go mad, plenty people do, especially feeble-
        minded people
I, for instance, want to have faith in the world like I used
        to have
Oh, I want to gratify all of my pathological desires!
I want to love every man and woman I see
I want to run up to little girls in the street and take
        their young bodies into my arms
When I pass the playground and see the little boys swinging
        in the swings and playing football in the park
I want to be the child that I never was
I want to have dirty hands and scratches on my knee where
        the Band-aid keeps slipping off
        and shining in my eyes, among the garbage cans
        of my birthplace
The clear light of sunrise!

But I am in this country illegally
In fact in birth to fetus accident
I cannot sit or stand or lie down in peace because the red
        hair of the fox is woven into my green garment
Spaded and shaded
By a candle in the moon so dim
I crouch over the ocean injecting ink into the lives
        of my contemporaries
Bootlegging feats of sheer witchcraft for crude bread and such —
Judging and waiting.

II

It is astounding how thoroughly policed the skin-forged
        boundaries are –
Scribbled on the underground subway advertisements, it is
        not *la rouge baiser* that makes Frenchwomen
So French
        it is "n i g g u h f i l t h"
King Kong
Mau Mau
Liver-lip ape
Rhythm Blues and Jazz
From Alabama to the Congo to Glasgow
Night train is the BLACK train.

III

If you are in the You Know Who it is easy to cop out in Europe
It is alright to drill a hole in your skull and avant-garde
        into childfoolery and senility
Plenty people do, especially babies, and once upon a time who
        sang a protest song
William Blake, for instance, has been appropriated to read his
        poems naked in Hyde Park this summer
Yevtushenko refused to know whence cometh his fame on the
        zoo stages of the West
        as his brother writers rot in jails
But I will never abandon the suffering of the suffering people!

Bessie Smith murdered on the Alabama pavement when blood of
        my mother's womb spewed out a paterless name.

Oh, I am in this world without a passport to humanity!
Shaded and spaded
I smoke hashish everyday and walk the street with ears
        full of eyes,

a love supreme
a love supreme
Every night I get stoned in the Seven Stars among the wretched
     of the earth
     and plot the downfall of empires.

END

✳ ✳ ✳

Game Life, London, 1967

To Colin MacInnes

In London
I do not know what a poem is
Perhaps I never knew
Even in New York
I found it difficult
To make things move,
To see them move,
To get the feeling
Beyond the noise
Of motor vehicles running inside of mouths
And science vibrating from within jukeboxes
Over the ballistics of the cash register
Muffled, perhaps, by the politics of total animation:
     To get to the feeling
     That people were actually alive.

From Third Avenue to Dalston Junction
I cannot get a poem to function!
Stoned without hope
Sober without power —
In London I have learned to expect
What is to be expected.

In my London neighborhood which is not my
neighborhood
I sit in the Free House For Public Drinking
Trying to connect anything with anything.
I want to run up to the people
And embrace them
I want to let them know
That they are dying —
From Bow Road to Piccadilly Circus
The West Indians work on the buses:
      Eny mo Faires, pleaase!

The particular Free House For Public Drinking
In which I sit
Is located on the King's Road
Outside, through the window, misty rain
Falls to pavement
Such lovely pavement so clean
For days of doom to scrounge upon —

In the Free House For Public Drinking
Thick red carpet immaculate beneath my feet,
Weavers and planters and sowers
In the glass frame
Bending, leaning, standing slightly
In positions of motion but not moving
In proximity of hay, field, and trees
In the painting on the wall.

If I move from my place in this chair
At this small round table
I would move to no one
If I rose, or gestured
Perhaps to smile, and say a prayer
I would disturb the lifeless clock hanging
Over the door below the runaway slave advertisement

I would aggravate the delicate balance
Of carefully behaving like furniture —
For prayer would be vulgar
In this spacious and lovely tomb.

Thirteen lavatories
At Notting Hill Gate Underground
Thirteen English gentlemen zip their trousers down:
> *But they cannot straightly pee*
> *For eyeballing me!*

I want Charles Dickens
To break out of Dartmoor prison
And take a look at the girls and boys
So beautifully deformed and buried
In the moors,
Chalk faced ladies who are preserved
And vanquished —
Now that the fields are fully enclosed
In generations of factories and wars
The charred slime in the lung
Of the English setter perched
With pipe and Virginia tobacco
Hallucinating lost empires built largely on black flesh —
Now that the treaties have all been signed
And broken
Now that Malthus is dead and Adam Smith is dead
And William Blake and the Stamp Act
And the First and Second World Wars
Are dead —
Now that the Memoirs contain nothing but kings doom
For the future, and the Queen on her throne
Is queen of men at pause:
> *Black man in the Free House For*
> *Public Drinking,*
> *Sit still and better not move!*

Sit without being
Be the absence of your presence
Be nobody in a room of pale ghosts
Persevering in fabricated dignity;
Stare, eyes you would weep,
At Icarus Jack soaring in the sky, sky
That is painted on the wallpaper glued to the
Paper wall —
Though walls are bombstones
Myth of Nations
Connecting generation to generation
In glorious tradition
Perpetuating perpetuation
Rope in British Museum round a chair
Polished daily
Canonizing tolerance and taboo,
Lords and Nobles, peasant, serf, war of roses,
Whenstoned Churchkill — alas,
The Gates are debris
On the ground;
But their names go marching on!
And I hear my soul whispering:
London is a lovely shrine.

* * *

Country

Glad
I know
What
My country
Done for me —
She
Big foot on gas pedal
Any country in the red

Bean of my eye —
Shit talking governments
Idiom idiots institutions
All the way from mississippi delta
To the river thames
Crazy legs
Be
Dangling from dead tree trunks
Wrecked by jet airplane crashes.
Anybody can get killed
Go on get yourself stoned
In the
East End,
Brixton
Porto Bellowing in the
Grove — some people deserve
To bomb St. Paul's Cathedral
Or
GO BACK ON DOLE —
Glad
I know
What
My country done for me
What I want to know

               What your country
               Done done for you?

Oberlin, Ohio: Later Work

from "CHATTANOOGA BLACK BOY" (1996)

I do not mean to downplay the role of racism in the making of my sense of who I am. But consciousness of myself as an African American is not all that constitutes my identity. Rather, humanity is the essential nature in which race, or having an African American identity, occurs or happens. And my identity is an ever-expanding process of discovering and becoming.

First and foremost I am a poet and writer. My identity as an African American does not determine what and how I write, unless I choose to make it so. Frequently I have chosen to write directly as an African American. Much of the rage I have felt for myself and for black people as victims of racism has been expressed in my writings. But neither my identity nor my writings are informed by racial experiences and feelings alone. I believe that identities founded on or rooted in exclusive notions of race are fallacious. Such identities diminish ourselves as well as the racial others who are excluded.

I recognize that people feel the necessity to embrace identities, and that identities are right and proper. Presently, identities based exclusively on race are a powerful urge in the world. But these identities are things that people invent, they are like garments people make, clothes they dress themselves in. But what is invented can be un-invented. That which is imposed can be resisted, subverted, uprooted, changed. To forge an identity and a consciousness that includes all other human beings, rather than excludes them, is an everlasting struggle in this world. But it can be done.

Low Down and Sweet

Here comes the sun
And I say it's allright
Your momma's momma
Your daddy's momma's momma
Your sister-in-law's momma
Your momma

Your uncle's cousin's momma's momma
Your niece's nephew's grandmomma's momma
Religious sanctified and holy momma ringing your black, veined
        hands and singing hallelujah and shouting up a storm
Sweet momma, chocolate momma
Throw lye in your face momma, mean momma, cross-eyed momma
Bow-legged momma, warm momma, gap-tooth momma,
          au naturel momma

Your momma
Your momma's main man's momma
Fat momma, snagged-tooth momma, your girl friend's momma
Your momma's momma-in-law, incestuous momma
Liver-lip momma
Good loving momma, tender momma, boogalooing in the
        after-hours joint

Your momma's sister's daddy's uncle's momma's great-great-
        grandaddy's momma's momma, 13th century African tribe
        woman's momma
Every-loving momma

High-yellow momma from the plantation tradition
Uncle Tom's momma, revolutionary momma, jive-ass momma

Childhood momma, senile momma, bulldigger momma, finger-
        popping juicy fruit chewing gum leave your children at
        home alone at night momma
Pregnant momma
Your momma

Your momma's momma
Ishmael Reed's momma
My momma, my grandmomma dead and crossed over Jordan

Welfare momma, drinking that good cheap wine and feeling
        no pain
Handkerchief head momma
Sapphire momma
Big black fat juicy momma with the meat shaking like jelly roll
        on your bones
Lean boney flat-chested momma with your legs like toothpicks
        standing on 125th Street in Harlem looking at the cop
        looking at you while doing finger nasties with his big
        black truncheon
Aunt Suzy's momma, Uncle Ben's and John the Conqueror's momma
Brer Rabbit's and Brer Fox's momma
Your momma

Goodtiming momma
Twotiming momma
Bigtiming momma
Swinging momma
Cold-hearted momma
Weak momma
Strong momma
No tooth momma
Gospel-singing momma
Funky momma, high-ass Mandingo momma, little cute walking momma

Tan, sepia momma stripped naked on the centerfold of
      Jet magazine

All!
Don't wear no draws.

   ✻ ✻ ✻

Hands

Reach! Put 'em up. Put your hands in the air.
On the other hand
Take your hands off of me.

Filthy hands, dirty hands, clean hands,
The end of the human arm, from wrist outward
Comprising the palm and the fingers;
Two-handed, underhanded, left-handed,
Right-handed, evenhanded; handy,
Handy man.

Handle. Something resembling a hand.
Hand-me-downs. Something like the pointers
On a clock or a style of writing, a person's
Signature. Put your hand to this seal,
A unit of linear measure, hand me that.
Look at his hands. Look, mother, no hands.

The hand that signed the paper fell a continent.
Five fingers on a scribbled pad.
Langston Hughes' hands!
Handsome. Handkerchief. Handbag. Handbill.
Handball. Handbook. Handcar. Handcuff. We
Must all do our best to help the handicapped.
Push that button. The hand of Tommie Smith.

"Dance like a butterfly and sting like a bee."
Braille, sorcery and magic, energy, vibrations,
Rays radiating power, gesture and personality.
Hands that make love, on the thigh, breasts,
Hot hands sending sensation, a handkissing
Man. Houdini's hands.
Bird in the hand. The size of a man's
Hand is the measure of his measure.

The hands of the sages, scribes, poets, scholars,
Political scientists thumb books, ransack archives,
Notate, hunt and peck, lecture and discuss.

Should a woman or man grind bones to make bread?
Painter, pianist, actor, surgeon, massage
My back.
The secretary's hands. Janitor's hands.
Handicraft. Handiwork. Hand organ. Hand gun.
Ready at hand, accessible, one or two bars
With which a bicycle or motorcycle is steered.

Fingerman, triggerman, conductor, fingerprints,
Manhandle. Get down on your hands and knees.
A manual laborer, the cards dealt to players
In a game, handout, greasy palms,
Help, aid, four functions and a thumb.
The hands of time. Hand me my slippers,
My pipe, my spectacles.

Reach! Reach for the sky, buddy. The sound
Of no hands are clapping. Ovation, encore, curtain
Call, digital, "up yours," like a red hot spear
The thumb of Nero came out of the sky and hung over
The fallen gladiator. Shoplifter. Hand lotion.
Caught with hands in the till. I got thirty-five
Hands out back, waiting, ready and willing to work.

Give me your hand. Shake on it.
You can't hand me that. What kind of handshake
      is that?

He had his hands under her skirt
And she had hers in his trousers.
All hands on deck! Hands across the border!
Hands off Latin America! Hands on the table!
Cold hands warm heart. On the corner the woman
Stands back on her legs and her hands on her hips.

Hand-to-hand combat. Hand in hand.
Few people can stand on their hands and even
Fewer can walk on their hands. Quick with her hands.
Sorry, but my hands were tied. The hand is quicker
      than
The eye. All join hands! Tomatoes that have not
Been touched by human hands. Toolmaker, fishermen,
Blacksmith, seamstress, planters, weavers and
      machinists.

Point! with the index finger.
Wave at the autumn leaves falling,
Drifting down from the trees to rest on the earth
In the wind like brown hands belonging
To brown people, grown old now and standing
In a crowd among themselves, willy nilly,
And the birds descend, swoop down out of the
Sky and slip up behind and cover the people's
Eyes with their wings.

Rites

How come he dont belong to nothing?
Where he born, where he work, what his sign —
Taurus, Aries, Scarecrow, Jupiter?
Makes no difference to him,
Shack up anywhere with anybody,
Be anything, accept anything, express
Anything, wear a woman's night gown —
Who's his friend, who's his enemy?

How come he wont stay in no certain place
Plant some roots, a family, raise a few
Younguns? Honest to God
Last I heard his ears flapping
Three sheets in the wind.

How come he wont step with the rest of us,
Fit in, act right,
What he believe in?
What his problem? If you ask me
He aint got no identity,
No fear of littleness
No anxiety of others, no dread of mortality,
No pride imploded chest vested behind
The ribs of some kind of group collectiveness —
A neighborhood, a nation, a race, fan of a
Favorite sport, a member of numbers bigger
Than individual.

Pin him down, classify him, categorize him,
Make him join the human race
Aint nobody *that* different
He cant be for real
Needs a stiff kick in the pants
Ought to be shot.

Ohio Myself

Ohio, I wear you like stepping into pants.

I am two hundred and eighty feet tall,
Three hundred and sixty three years old.
My silo legs stride across your ridges, lakes,
        rivers, flatlands,
I got on suspenders —
Polkadot blue red white striped woolen shirt
Open down my hairy chest

In the hind pocket of my longjohn trousers
An ear of your sweetest corn.

✳   ✳   ✳

Ohio Klan

White sheets
Hanging on a clothes line
Crucify the golden corn
Mark my stand
Against the sky
Silo flames —
Red in the night.

✳   ✳   ✳

Oberlin Negroes

Black people
In Oberlin Ohio
Still say
"Colored."

The white people
Don't know
What to say.

* * *

Oberlin, Ohio

Greetings
My name is Oberlin Ohio
People never heard of me
Mispronounce my name "Oberland"
But that's allright
Jump back jack.

I am a small town
In the north central part of Ohio
South of Cleveland where John D. got his start,
South of Wellington town of respite,
On highway #58 intersecting highway #10,
Flanked by the town of Elyria and the city of Lorain
Red dust city of bellowing industrial furnaces
Lining Lake Erie shore, low rain city
Second largest Puerto Rican population
In the nation
Jump back jack.

Oberlin Ohio
A pretty good old soul
Between two traffic lights
Four streets get in and out of me
Two supermarkets, two barber shops, two drug stores
Three banks, one restaurant, two laundromats
Three carry-out pizzerias, a convenient late night
Delicatessen, an expensive clothing store,
One motel named "Oberlin Inn," a co-op bookstore

A courthouse, a single-room police station
A brand-new fire building two blocks
On the outskirts of me
Churches of all denominations
Black White Integrated
Methodist Presbyterian Catholic
Congregationalist Rural Pentecostal
But no city storefront Holy Rollers
And nursing homes aplenty
Get the picture
That's allright
Jump back jack.

A railroad used to run through me
Black-topped now and paved over
I am a dry town
Governed by a city council
The manager of which is hired according to
Qualifications —
I say
"Jump back jack"
Because I am a town of folk settlement
Since 1833 until now
My founder was Johann Friedrich Oberlin
Pioneer, humanitarian, man of God, smoked no pipe
Drank no gin, seldom went out at night —
I am a tradition of liberalism in the heartland
Of Middle America
My heritage is the Underground Railroad
The rescuing of runaway slaves, the settling
Of whom constitute half of my population
Admittedly small, some few thousand black
And white souls, I loom large as a town of racial
Peace and prosperous living —
In my center stands Oberlin College
Famed for high excellence, musical genius and

Liberal tendencies
First institution of higher learning to admit
Women, Negroes and intersexual living before
Any other in the nation
Area code 216
Phone number 775 8121
Jump back Jack.

Notables touch my ground
19th century newspapers, military documents,
Federal census schedules, city directories,
Westwood cemetery records, archives and
Histories of surnames alphabetically ordered
John Brown Jr., Elisha Gray, George Frederick
Wright, Rebecca and James Harrington, listed as
"James Herndon" in the 72nd U.S. Colored Infantry
(Company A)
Simpson and Catherine Younger, children of
Charles Younger uncle of the outlaw brothers
Enlisted in the 27th U.S. Colored Troops
(Company A)
Five feet five inches tall, light complexion —
Free blacks Lewis Sheridan Leary husband
Of Langston Hughes's grandmother Mary Patterson
John Mercer Langston himself resided on
East Lorain Street
John Anthony Copeland of the famed Wellington Ohio
Fugitive slave rescue by Oberlin citizenry
Leary Copeland and Shields Green enlisted with
John Brown at Harper's Ferry
An obelisk bears their names in Vine Street Park
Memorial cemetery —
My music conservatory produced great composers
Symphony directors
Though Paul Robeson never sang in me
Jazz went to college here and in 1953

Dave Brubeck took his famous five
Frank Lloyd Wright left a sketch pad in the attic
Of a house he built here
And in 1978 the first black woman to manage a city
Jump back jack!

Jump back
And do not play me cheap
Do not give me any wooden nickels
Do not try to push any twenty dollar bills
With your picture on them.

Greetings
Oberlin Town
Zip Code 4 4 074
That's me
Well and alive
In the north of Ohio
Jump back jack.

✳   ✳   ✳

The Tap House, South Main Street, Oberlin Ohio

The only joint inside of city limits
A railroad box car
Three point two beer
Sucker-size pool table
25¢ pieces ready for the slot
Heads or tails denote who's up next
Indescript cue-sticked
Phalanxes of would-be Minnesota Fats
In a one-horse town

Aggregate outside, mill around
Motorbike jocks, punk handlebars,

Whistling, cat-calling, boisterous jousting
Smoke pot,
Ferocious bulls crumple plastic beer cans barehandedly
Inside they congregate
Jukebox blasting Rolling Stones
Chug-a-lug, chug-a-lug all night long
Shout bellicose malediction maleficent
Rear back, exhibit ball and penis baskets
Scratch crotches, exude sex in Levi denim
Buttock crevices flex arse muscles, teenmen
Boymales at work on the masculinity
Of their manhood.

Like rat-infested hold below
Descend stairs, graffito john stink of urine
Ammoniated excrement stained bits of newspaper
Unflushed prophylactic vomit Juicy Fruit
25¢ french tickler, thrill her, drill her
Kill her stay hard forever guaranteed.
Razor-slit booths, sagged seats along
Dimly lit walls
Soda-pop beer spilled on aged formica tables
Overturned ashtrays, fingerprints, bits of Frito Lays
Peanut shells, barbecue chips.

Behind bar's length greasy apron gout-gut bartender
Bending grunting,
Back-room kitchen hamburger, french fries,
Painting of seagulls above the grill.

The floor is spit on worn wood
Inside a railroad boxcar cigarette butts,
Crumpled napkins, burnt matchsticks
Months of muddy shoeprints
Sackcloth curtains drawn tightly over front
Glass window blacking out the light

Sound of pinball bowling machines
Pac man in dimly lit atmosphere
Creating warmth, heat of bodies
Loud friendliness good-natured recreation
Black and white happy days,
A few older men and women spotted in the crowd
Some college students hovering in booths
Enjoy the fun of night life in small town
Midwest America
Pool table dominated by afro jeri curls
And every minute rolling rock blasting hillbilly
Country western turns to smokey robinson b b king
Soul funk ohio players rhythm blues and donna summer
Disco.

Enter Tanya
Five feet eight inches tall female midwest stock
In bright blue rayon dress making love to flesh
With every knee-length swish
bleached little girl bobbie curls sheltering
Pushed back in mind memory of childhood rape
Incestuous father, brother
A slender structured face laced with alcoholic
Restraint,
Mascara eyelash unpainted kissable lips unkissed
Slim frame, lean body, older than girl younger than
Woman, measured self-countenance tight held looseness
Almost snobbery
Noble is Tanya
Through the crowd which parts for her majesty
Quickly rapid bird-walk hillbilly elegance,
A worm strangled in the fist of her center
May the Lord bless her soul.

Tanya knows the pool table is not a bed made of water
The pool table is a gangrene sky

Stretched over four legs of ox
Cloven feet, hooves gothic as succotash sauerkraut
Gothic as barrelhouse country and western
Gothic as cabbage
Barbarous as peasant woman holding handle of hoe
Bent squat poor white trash against
Ohio landscape of agrarian poverty
Turn classical in the Tap House Queen of the green
Tanya
Right finger bridge
Left hand stick
Drive through six pockets
Queen of the green
Persona of march
Stretch, reveal rayon moons sensuous female regal
Inside of a railroad box car
25¢ worth of saturdaynight sociality
Bless her soul.

✻   ✻   ✻

Oberlinian Quartet

I

Ella Johnson
You are sunflower
Whose asking is shaped like mine.

In this small town of fresh air
Fouled by rumor
Heads stuffed with gossip
Your lack of well being
The state of your estate
Chiseled lines in the deep of your face
Pants empty of a man's leg
A man's stand

Sprung door hinge
Roof shingles needing repair
Dead light bulb in the basement
Of your lonely heart
In this lovely town of green rodents.

II

Ella Johnson
Crowded aloof
The ritual feast
The ceremonial white
The ham and cheese and champagne
Cornered against wallpaper
In this hall of bride and gloom
There language of the body
Silently cry.

III

Ella Johnson
Long of legs
Tall as sunflower
In Oberlin Town
You are the only woman
Whose asking is shaped like royal gown.

Womanly
In woman's outfit
You are womansome
In the 7:30, eight and nine o'clock
Of blackness
I may approach empty of nothing
Shaped in desire full of song
Whose asking ripe sweat and sweet
Is yours and mine.

IV

Ella Johnson
Brown of skin
You are Mammy Pleasant
Your own fence you can mend
Change your own light bulb
Trim your own hedges
Put your own legs into your own pants.

Amazon androgyny draped in Zora Neale Hurston attire
Scarcely brimmed hat crescentwise
Expensive wool skirt
Slit knee pleat to where calves are full
Wide-lapel suit jacket gabardine shirt
Marie Laveau high cranium
Crane's neck in purple ascot of elegant satin.

Ella Johnson
Brown of skin
Long of legs
Stately statue handsome and regal
Sculpture of your thighs
Splendor of your hips
Noble, sensuous, exquisite
In small hours of this small Ohio town
You are sunflower atop African mound
The only woman in city limits
Whose asking is shaped like mine.

Boatwoman
Warrior of rain gods
Sister of my mother's tribe
Ella Johnson
Animal of being.

The Point

It is where you shall be begrudged and beguiled,
It is the place, time and circumstance of your origin,
and it is the source of your most ardent pursuit.
It is September 1970, the year of moon and honey,
Get in your red automobile and head one block South
to Lorain Street which is Ohio State highway #10,
Turn left and ease on down the road destined in the
direction of The Point.

Pause and reflect
Look straight down highway #58,
See the captured runaway rescued by the two halves of the
town of Oberlin in process —
Do not continue down that road! Do not follow that procession!
Do not go to Wellington!

Pause and reflect.
For the point is more than the leaning men and their laughter
and the drinking . . .

Here they come, the old, the young, the fisherman with his
homemade reel . . . the silent one with his bag of cigarettes,
the federal aviation boys with the wreckage of jet
airplanes in their brains, the three friendly pigs of Oberlin
and the one poet in whose breast an agony bleeds from a
secret universality among the dogs of the point and by
every living beast in the devil damned town . . .

Night Letter to John A. Williams

(4 a.m., est.)

Out of print
is a book with no pages
nothing but silence
that like a spark struck
in the dark
dimly fades.

Where are
The sons of light
The flashings back, the night's song, and
The captain blackmen of all valor
Where is the tongue who cried I am!

Ours is a predicament of paradox
a heritage of shark teeth
eyesights, eardrums and black hunger
shredded like confetti by
the mammon moloch.

Out of print
is like a book with no binding
nothing but the rustling sound of
        autumn leaves
falling to ground
outside a lonely lit window.

The typewriter's harvest, the aching
back, the high blood pressure of literacy
trees that would fly are
shackled in stockhouses of remainder
scream as they burn

as they are poisoned by the
    american death
and drop like starved cattle.

Shall we marvel at this sight
Or shall we write!

*   *   *

Crossing Brooklyn Bridge at 4 O'Clock in the Morning, August 4th, 1979

Oh, love spat upon and made mockery of!

The night's sorrow
This heart of moon tears in the darkest before sunrise
This aloneness after betrayal
Dust blown grit of yesterday rot
This suffocating thirst
This ache to plunge into oblivion!

I, shoulder hunched, hands balled into my pockets,
    shivering in the cold,
Stand at this time morning facing the Bridge of Brooklyn
    leading across into Manhattan,
My bridegroom feet covered in running shoes torn
    by nails of jilt,
My legs of lactic acid, my knees weakening upon the grates
    of the bridge,
My gin eyes, drooped as the lowering of curtains
    around the one who is dying,
Peer down into the waters of absolution
    and scream your name,
Walt Whitman! Walt Whitman! Walt Whitman!

Poet of ferry boats and of poets ages hence to come,
Wound dresser, washer of the slave's feet,
Dream keeper who sleeps with prisoners in slumber,
Oh, nurse of eternal compassion!
Ferry me across these waters of deceit.
Bear me safely over this bridge of steel and concrete
That I may live to shed this grief.

*   *   *

A Cat by Any Name

For Amiri

grandmother used to say cats can
see spirits and are capable of
walking one inch above the ground

well, a cat's a cat for a that.

i first met him in five spots
third avenue and st. marks place
i was with my fisherfellow friend pastor
of the neohoodoo church
i recollect the night:

speaking in a voice pleasingly quiet
"i am the griot of cats," he said
"i possess the alchemy of *pantomimus,* i know
            the mojo of bags full of puns, i turn myself
            into loud roaring, i do it all the time
            i have never been a kitten, i have always
            been a bob cat."

oh, he was a cat for a that allright
and a he cat was he.

but in his grandpa's cabin there
were many rats
no hausa warrior from the north came
down and slew the mean dogs who chased
him and bit his behind
no ebo patriarch, nor spider trickster
put things back together that fell apart.

but he had a mind full of bags
and a sack full of names
among the tenements of the metropole
he beat the drums of jihad
he conjured black fire on white paper
he swallowed swords and spewed out brimstone
he rared up on hind legs and roared like
a subway train

oh, he was a terrible cat for a that!

he kidnapped lightning, handcuffed thunder
wrote his autobiography on gravestones and put
the dead on a wonder

he worked on it night and day
shovelling coal in dante's inferno
a name for dhis and a bag for dat
a bag over hyear and a name over dhare
catman amiracle swahili pseudonymous rex
a name in need a name indeed!
nine times nine
in cat's eyes
oceans of jade
rush and rise
hyear me talking to ya
ever seed amazing grace by the
yellow glow of moon dance on a black

cat's throat
zig-zag a streak of pure light
and hightail up a tree

well, a cat's a cat for a that too.

look, look!
along the thoroughfare people are waving
to him
proletarian cat
stridently stepping in a mayday
parade
"that's my husband, that's my husband!"
his wife throws him a basket full
of kisses.

* * *

Grenada, October 1983

To Dessima Williams

Island of New Jewel.
Sun!
Where sun shines no more.

October was your month of dying
Out of flying machines
Jackals of death
Descend from the sky.

Oh, Grenada!

Island of laughter
Where laughter died.

Your jewels shall sparkle anew.
Over the world
your laughter shall fly!

*   *   *

Stars Bleed

Angola
Mozambique
Namibia —
How do stars bleed?

Do they
Hang their heads
And cry?

Or
Do they flame
Red —

Thunder and fire
In an African sky!

*   *   *

Michael Stewart — Enunciation

Michael.
Sun from whose fire
Stars are born.

New york city subway is the darkest hole in
   the
World.

I heard silence scream like jackals
In the slots of turnstiles on the night
You were beaten into spinach
And ground under heels.

If only I were insane I could believe what they
Said, "comatose cardiac arrest,"
Mark a tick in the
Box, "isolated incident," and abandon you for
Dead. Make no mistake they were men not
    women
Who sent your head down concrete steps
Like a cabbage bouncing on a yoyo string.

September 15 1983
Hurrah for the iron whale fleeing through the
    hole
In the world!
As your wrists were squeezed tight into cuffs
And your ankles bound, I saw crucifix
Advertisement on the platform wall. Make no
    mistake
They were not women but men dressed in
    dungeon blue
Wielding a mad mob of truncheon penises,
A pogrom of shattered teeth, dislocated
Shoulders, damaged spinal cord, ruptured
Eye sockets, graffito on calvary.

If only I were mute as forty witnesses were
Mute, I would glue my tongue over my eyes
    and
Believe you ripped out your own insides and
Disposed them in the trash.

But I am loud as pain, and I am here to
Sound your name, Michael, *Michael!*

Men, not women, ravished and killed you.

The Red Crab Gang and Black River Poems (1999)

from **ONE: The Red Crab Gang**

To Groesbeck Parham MD

1.

> Red
> Tell me how shall I work thee
> I work thee one by one,
> I work thee two by two,
> And I work thee three by three

In the journey of life there comes a junction where every person's biography turns into a battleground of good and evil, skeletons of hope cast shadows of despair and in the afternoon red dread inhabits the air, makes the weather terribly unfair

> The dying of the light
> In the evening
> At the crack of night
> Red moon rider
> *Monsieur Le*
> *Rouge*
> Comes into town

> Warlock wizard
> Red spider crab crawls
> In and out of hospital rooms
> From
> Bed to bed
> Webbing
> Dead to dead

2.

Tell me how shall I work thee
I work thee one by one

      I work thee cold autumn morns
      When the red crab gang declares
      Lethal demand and causes
      Insatiable desire

      To inhale the fumes
      Of hell's fire
      That infects the
      White cells, as the
      Nicored brain
      Loses its train

    Monsieur
      Le
       Rouge

       Formally:
       Red Stetson hat
       Silk red suit
       Deadly red eyes
       Crimson red cravat
       Day glow shades

Burgundy shoes and red cigar
    Vertebrate
    Straight
    Legs
Dis Connected Feet
Dis Membered Shadow
      In red district
      Of red lit night

                    Lean against
                    Red lamp pole
In red fog
Of Nicotine
Towns —

                    ✳   ✳   ✳

                         3.

    In the evening
    Mister Red, alias
    Nicotine Nicored
    In the evening, alias
    Nicored Nicotine
                         Before sun
                         Go down
                         Red came into
                         My body's healthy town
                         Of solid ground,
Spewing red hell
Through back doors opening
Onto red streets —

            In
       Amos Tutuola Town
                         Trees walk
                         Backward
                         Red grazes on
                    Green lawns, and
                         Turns them red
   In
   Tutuola Reds Town
   Clocks Telephones,   Letters catch fire
                           In red mail boxes
                               Of impeccable charm;

"ISHMAEL REED"
                    Stenciled in red ink
                    On every building wall

          Fire hydrants
          And
          Fire engines
          Squall
Still life
Red eggs red rice
In darkest night
White beets in
The iron rice bowl of China,
Sit there
In Russia red square

                    Oh, white sheets drying
                    On wire lines
                    Redden
                    By sunlight dying
E-y-e . . . e-y-e . . . e-y-e . . . e-y-e . . . say
In the evening, the
Evening   Before bright
                    Sun demise
                    Red moon rise, and
                    Red rock
                    Rocks
                    In red
                    Rocking chair

Oh, silver moon rise
Please rise —
          Rise over
          Chattanooga bed spread of
                    Tennessee clay, where
                    The mother lay

149

Dead,
The mother lay
Dead
The mother is dead

＊ ＊ ＊

7.

The   Red
The   Red
How shall I work thee
I work thee two by two

Red hospital
     Ambulances
     Convey
     Saturday night
     Razor neck
     Triage

Bloody red uniform
Doctor
Nurse
Intern

Red
Tile floor line
Red theatre
Bone nerve and tissue

Red alert!
     Forceps
     Suction
     Sutures
     Bandages

Red alert!
　　Over New Orleans
Red alert!
　　Over Baton Rouge
　　　　Catwalk queen
　　　　Red silk gown
　　　　Velvet
　　　　Sheets, and
　　　　Pillows of
　　　　Red feathers

Shall we tarry
Shall we make love

Oh so redly
Streams of setting sun
Filter through windows
Making the lace curtains glow —
Shall we inhale the red
On this hospital bed

Or shall we die
Of eating
Too much
Apple pie — ?

Shall we
Dream
Red dreams
Wear red
Underwear
Talk red talk
With unred
People, and blow
Red poison
In their faces

Shall we settle
　　Or move along?

11.

Early
Morning
Before dawning
Red yawning.

          Compared to the Gang
          Of Green
          The Red Crab Gang
          Is *Mean*

Lumpectomy
Hysterectomy
Cervical Red
Bone
    Marrow

          Nicored killer thug
          Carcinoma assault
          Blood bank hold up
          Red crab gang deadlier
          Than
          The gang of green

Women of unusual height dress themselves in gowns of white — red
gloves, red slippers, and slap faces of doctor men red as velvet carpet in
ruling class delicatessen, the red crab gang eats
          Women of unusual height
          Requiring mammograms
          Ductile Carcinoma in Situ
          Minimally invasive squamous cells

When
Red
Crab moon
Comes

His   Calamity   Raising hell
                                                In red
                                                Infect the light
                                                Of sun

                        *   *   *

                        14.

Red was the color
Of Nicored's breath
Hair
Red as an autumn dawn, as
                        Leaves in
                        New England —

                                        Today red
                                        Tomorrow gone

Remorse and sorrow
Nicored puffing
Jowls tarred and
Burning
                        In winter cloudy days
                        Naked red leaves
                        Crisp under foot,
                        Trampled into ground
                                        Then gone
                        Red mustache
                        Lower lip nicored
                        Loved dead
                        A still life
                        For the prize:
Ripe red Cherokee apples
Carrots, big red oranges
And grapes

Leap from
The red bowl
Of his heart and
Kiss her dead South Carolina lips
Long neck bend,
Red not, love makes
The universe
Spin

Chattanooga
Red
Tennessee
Clay
Georgia
Red
Sod
Squishy
Beneath
Naked feet
Between
Naked toes
The red damp
Clay
Clings
To kneeling
Knees, and tears
Tumble down
Red cheeks
Fertilize the
Wife grave —
Kiss the wife tombstone
Red taste of South Carolina clay
The embalmed odor
Of marinated death
In the steam heat
Of this red summer —

15.

              Jamaica tranquil
                                  Hills
                                  Mountain water runs
                                  Herbs grow wild greenly

Go
Tell
Jah
                          Volcano red
                                  Lava down
                  Furrows of
                  Mountains
                  And
              Fertilize wet
                  Beds
                  Of
              Herbs growing
Tell Jah
Blood flows,
In the night, through
Red memory
Of the light

                                  Tell Jah
                                  Tell Jah
                                  Tell Jah

              Unlock the lock
              Unred the dread
              And
              Undread the dead
              In red
              Tell
              Jah

She mother
    Is
Not going to walk
    In Jerusalem just like John

        She mother's name
           Is
        Not going to dwell
           In Rastaland

Oh, tell Jah
The mother's real name
The wife's real name
    Is
Dread, I and I Woman
    Is
Jah, I and I Woman

In skies of red sun
Spread
Red rays
Of cockpit
    Light

Oh, Jah!
    The light the light the light the light the
Light is the mother's name
The wife's name
If they die
They live again —
        Oh Jah! Oh Jah!
        Grasp our hands
        Jah,
        The bruised blood
        Of the mother son
        Of the father wife
        Oh, Jah

Blood
Fingers
Probe avenues of
The body,
Seek out the
Carcinoma red gang
Confront the life
Eating
Crabs

Oh Jah!
Oh Jah!
Oh Jah!
         Make the sun burn
Oh Jah!

         Make it shine
         All night long.

from **TWO: Black River Poems**

To Bruce Weigl

Black River

River of the black
What men and women used to be
Is not what they are today.

Black River make my blood tingles
Make my flesh shivers.

Blood, water of the ocean
Flesh, foliage of the sea
River of the black
You ain't what you used to be.

River of the black
Running underneath
Overpasses
Running underneath
Railroad tracks
River of need
River of lack
Crusty bottom
Dead weed.

Black River
Make my blood tingle.

Beautiful is the land
Beautiful are the fields
Turning mills
Ten thousand wheels

Ganglion silos outstretch
Golden flowers of the sun
In shade of muse red barns, and
Kill the lovely hills.

Black River
Make my flesh shiver.
Down the gully listlessly
Hot winds roam,
Cane sugar corn sweet,
A woman full grown stands
In the center of her own
Farm —
Image of that woman upon the fields.

But look back!
River of the black,
Is that an eyeball
Tumbleweeding down your calcified crevice?
Is that a limb? a corn cob?
A mother's arm clinging babe
To breast?

Shivering flesh.
Black river
Is that a criminal?
Skull fractured,
Nose smashed,
Resisting arrest?
Is that my heart willy-nilly floating
Like a broken twig
In stagnant water?

Blood Tingles
River of the black.
Freckled face,

Freckled shoulders,
Honey suntanned —
The lone woman stands
In the center of the path
Leading to her house, casting
Casting a shadow of my spirit.

Sweating palms.
Present,
Future, past —
Thanks for every breath you breathe
It may be the last —

Black River
Crusty bottom
Dead weed
River of lack
River of need
What men and women used to be
Is not
What they are today

River of the black
Rejuvenated waters
Make your soul
Fly away

* * *

Ohio Listening

It's autumn in Ohio
Things to be done
Visit the doctor
Before leaves fall.

Autumn in Ohio
Black birds southward bound
Darkening the sky
North winds congregate
In fields of dry stalks
A loose shingle rattling
On the roof.

Autumn in Ohio
Repairs to be made
Firewood to gather
Loved ones to hold
Before the leaves turn gold
And the hawk descends
Formidable cold.

* * *

Portrait of a Poet

People stop me along the street
They think I am James Baldwin
James Baldwin is dead

People in a crowd seek me out
They think I am Ralph Ellison
I am not

At the literary reception
People think I am Zora Neale Hurston
Zora Neale is dead

I am not James Baldwin
I am not Ralph Ellison
I am not Zora Neale Hurston

Perhaps when dead
People will think I am
Moby Dick

Only the Black River knows
Only the river knows

Previously Unpublished Poems

You Take a Country Like America

I know every man's got blood in his veins
Deep in the heart of every woman a lantern burns.
It took me a lot of complaining to discover
This mystery.

You take a name like *love*
Or a word like *America*.
I take them in my hands and crush them,
I press the crumbs in the wiry hair of
My chest.

But look at my face —
Watch the way I stand —
I knew a girl named Ann
Every taxi driver in town layed her body
In the dirt (they said).
When she died I cried like a dog.
I knew a big lad
He had twelve years of education
And the prettiest girl in the world
He went away and fought a war against "aggression,"
He came back to be lynched in Mississippi.

You take a country like *America*
Or a feeling like *love*,
I plant them into the good earth,
And wait.

Poor Mildred's Delicatessen

All the way from South Carolina to Rockefeller Plaza
The schizoid spots flash on and off
The fish in the flesh
Eat way the marrow in the cracks . . .

Poor Mildred! — Jersey Turnpike is a long ways back
The unlocked door slams loud
Third Avenue whores urinate in dark places
And Jesus Christ comes down from Connecticut
Every weekend.

The past will trap us all. It will haunt us.
The privies standing in Carolina peach orchards —
The bellies of fish litter that grave yard behind your house,
Unlock the corridors of something mysterious within you.

Bury that thing beneath your doorstep
Emit it from you, and kiss it, and good-bye —

Poor Mildred! — all the way from Isabelle, from Joe,
From Brother and Mama and Alfonzo, and Evelyn — and
Pearl, the jewel.

Up-town, they run hot iron through your hair,
Down-town, all that suffering curls up again.
Poor Mildred! — you've got one Ace in the hole,
And soon He will fall from His high place, forever.

Calvin Hernton Seeks to Build and Preserve a House

To Mildred

I

Where shall the monument begin
Upon what foundation
How shall the True House be erected?

Now you are going away
I will miss you, I will be lonely,
I will worry and know sleepless nights
So terrible
I shall walk dark streets
Sit in darker places
And drink   and brood.

After having pressed my mouth to yours
Lived each breath of your breathing
After having been told that I am loved
After having loved,
In so short a space within confines so desolate,
Now that you are leaving
I shall walk quietly into a church
Kneel there before the altar
And pray.

II

How shall love's monument begin?
Upon what foundation shall it be erected?
Christ died but on the third day he rose.

The True House is the Temple of God
It is built upon the foundation of the Rock.
The True Temple is the *family.*
Love is the rock.

The first and last, the indivisible, the
Ever prevailing, undisputable
Rock!

III

Once erected
How shall the Temple be preserved?
I have seen men curse God   in God's name.
I see a world filled with haters.
I see people dancing a dance who have forgotten
          the meaning, or twisted it
Beyond its Truth.
I hear confused, hopeless tongues uttering
          hopeful words.

How shall the Truth be preserved?
Now that you are leaving
I shall be alone.

IV

Tell them the Temple is based upon
A solid foundation
Tell them the True House of God is created out of
          love and marriage!
Conceived by children
Through the placing-on of lips in nights soft as
          the fur of freshly born kittens
Tell them the True Temple is not
          an organization for the purpose of self-aggrandizement
Or national expediency —
The family is a religious institution.

And when you depart from me, my love,
Remember,
> take this monument with Thee
> forget not the altar, where the candle of
Resurrection flickers about the profile of my
> tearful face.

V

And remember!
Once erected, even then the True House
Is not so easily preserved. For
There are those, envious, begrudging,
Of the house,
> unbelievers, who stand without, that
Will strive, will strike out boldly
> or cowardly
Against the True Temple.
Those who for various and often unscrutinized motives,
Those who, while standing upon the Rock, will oppose
> and offend,
Those who will strive to arrest and destroy

The one Truth.
The only House.

VI

Shall I grieve?
You know grief will be mine.
You know I love you committedly and will
> suffer during your absence
Remember!
The True House is the True Temple
I love you
> and want to marry.

The True Temple
The Rock
The Cathedral
Must be built from within
It will prevail against those who oppose
        from without
        against those who offend.
It must be built on Love.

This is the way it must be erected
This is the way it begins
This is the way the family will survive

This is the monument.

*   *   *

When Broomriders Black

These days when broomriders black
Hammer hell's teeth into bigged doorknobs,
Blues and news come bent broke bearing
Tales of ash gray stumps in fields
Where neither burnt earth nor ghost waters
Give forth tears
To weep for me and my country.

Oh Lord, I tuned my nerves in your fires
And made a marriage, I fashioned my axe
On your anvil and built a house, I drove that axe
Into my maid's head and forked forth a child.

Now bad luck thrones my mail box
Wired brains strung on poles ejaculate
Wrecked freight trains throughout all the cities
There is rumor of famine by drought and floor

There is whisper of strangulation by seavines,
Hail, then, deadeyed tyrant, ascend!
Sword every child born dead,
Devolve sickness upon the family,
Devolve debt, devolve guilt.

Now oh, Lord, make me the pig iron of your mercy!
Prayers causing God lift up your fist
And heave the knockout lick to this acid regime.

＊　＊　＊

Deep Sea Blues

Lord, I've had nothing but
The blues
Since my baby's been gone —
Since my baby's been gone,
I've had those deep sea blues.

The day she left
I didn't shed a tear,
Now I've got those deep sea blues
She ain't been gone but a year.

Every night I wrap myself
In a long white sheet,
Every night wrap my self
In a long white sheet,
Lord, I cry for my baby's body
I cry myself to sleep.

Well, I'm going down to the river,
Gonna do what I should —
Lord, I'm gonna jump in the river,
Cause my baby's done gone for good.

Since my baby's been gone —
Deep sea blues,
Since my baby's been gone,
I've had nothing but
The blues.

* * *

Id and Ego

White folks in public park
Stare like I'm
     some kind of spark
From a way-off star.

I ain't no star —
I'm black as they are.

* * *

1961
(*Time past contained in time future* — T. S. Eliot)

Going . . .
New news and old blues
Goodbye memories
Hello news
Goodbye blues —
Old news and new blues

             Goodbye and hello

Memories . . .
Cast off worn clothes
In the winter wind stand
Unbeaten,

Head thrown back like an egoist:
Vision burning within
My soul —

                    Might and memory!

This season
The struggle will strike at the quick.

* * *

Southern Laughter

Laughter!
Laughter from the throats
Of folks
Who know nothing
But pain and misery.

Laughter in the night,
In taverns and juke boxes
And midnight strip teasers,

Laughter on the street corner
In one last pair of dirty overalls —
Laughter in the withered corn fields
Lying between the skinny legs
Of some naked woman's body —
And laughter
From the bastard mouths of
Mulatto babies.

Sex laughter . . . messed up in corn liquor —
Corn liquor and whores,
And poverty and disease and babies
And fear and race hatred,

All messed up in sill-sick laughter —
And no crop to harvest when the harvest time come.

Laughter . . . Laughter . . . Laughter . . . and more laughter!

Lord . . . every time I hear that
Southern laughter

* * *

Statement

For the class of 1954, Talladega College

Out there in the cold, cruel world
Where there is neither glow of warmth
Nor breath of love,
They knock on you, beat on you,
Step on you, kick on you, kill you
Deader than a doorknob —
Throw you in a mud hole
And God-*damn you!*

* * *

Black Metathesis

Your heads are full of
Air-plane crashes
Your eyes are cataracted with
Soot and smoke and debris and dead
Babies from the bombed cities!

> Black did not bomb those cities!
> Black did not wreck all those air-planes!
> Black did not beat up all those Negroes!
> Black did not set fire to that alarm clock!

Black is not in the insurance business!
Black did not stand by while the helpless
woman was being murdered!

Black is *Elemental*, is cosmological
Swirling, crying, emanating, laughing
Descending, bending, sauntering, caressing
Like a nude black girl in her black lover's arms

Black makes the sun come through the cracks
And warms this lonely place

Black *is* —
And God made light out of
Some of it

* * *

Hank Dixon and the Law

The law!
You asked me to respect the law
You speak about the *spirit* of the law, the *concept*
of justice, freedom, truth, fair play, and the
sacredness of institutions . . .
Fishbone in a rattlesnake throat!

I give you a valley of dead bodies shot down by the law
I show you ten million shanty-town tenement ratholes and fifty million
starving babies: all perpetuated by the law and maintained
by the sacredness of institutions
I take you west and east, south and north, show you office
buildings, limousined socialwork robots, masturbating
justice and fair play, ejaculating corruption;
Frank Riverton, millionaire, stole five million from the
American public; gets "investigated," receives a

suspended sentence; is welcomed by Argentine dictators;
he loves humanity, is kind to children and deplores
juvenile delinquency
Willie Jones, a black peon in Alabama found an abandoned
bag of rotten cabbages; takes them home and family eats
a first meal in years; he is later "captured," and
sentenced to eight years at hard labor; he has a "record"
for the rest of his life and can't get a job anywhere
There can be no respect for the "concept" of law
apart from the *character* of its execution!

Do you remember Medgar Evers
What does the name Charles Mack Parker mean to you
Why do you think God is white
What does the deprivation of 25 million black people
bring to your mind

You talk about law and institutions!
What is your name!
Crime is for you who are the law
The law is for you who do not get caught
Institution is for you who make money out of oppression
and slaughter
The innocent and powerless are smeared and hunted down

I am no longer innocent,
I strap two gallons of petrol across my back, a zippo lighter in my belt,
and revolt
against the law
I will love depraved people with bitter memories and uncertain
futures
The law does not want truth
The law wants to be paid
The law gives us a mutilated baby wrapped in a bloody mantle!

A Lantern for Abigail Moonlight

To Nora Hicks and Ree Dragonette

The Jackal of the flesh howls in hollow of the mind
Jackal of the mind in hollow of night;
The moon drops low at the turning of black day,
        The Red cock cries out —
Goodwoman Sarah, you have been chosen!
Goodwoman Susanna, awake and do not awake!
The man in the British Museum no longer strives
Against sinister things;
He is dead and not arisen;
He is arisen and not dead —

Come then, let us oppose and be victimized;
Let us victimize and be opposed.

If there were no evil in the world how could men be
Certain there is good?
If evil did not exist women would have to create it.
In the crevice of dark dichotomies where flesh
Communes snakes and familiars
It is said there are sundry deeds perpetrated
By isolatable personage:
Those who are deformed and abnormal
Those who are hunchback and mysterious, those who are ugly and
        those who are extremely beautiful;
Those who wail and moan and fall down rolling and mouth
        foaming, those who oppose and victimize; those who are
        veiled about the face, and those whisper to no one
        and those who cry out to no one, and those who wear
        disguises of animal and those who kill by dart and ragdoll
        or by tongue of wolves or by birth of monsters, from
        wherein the fork falls —

All, according to the particular insanity of the times, to fits and
Tantrums and visions, according to affliction, to blindness
And to dumbness, in various stages of wretchedness and perfection;
According to individual responsibility for collective guilt
And collective error —
Accordingly, the isolated personage constitutes a threat to
　　convention, popular notions, custom, belief, order,
And must be sought out as villain, heretic, or hero.

Witches are rebellion against God's province
And God's province is whatever we who are in power
　　say it is

Therefore, I saw Sarah Good, in a stealthy manner, comming
Out of the Divel's Din, with cat and handle of
Broom, riding down on my body as I lay asleep,
I yelled and I kicked,
But no sound came from my mouth, no motion came from
　　my limbs;
And Sarah Good, the witch, assumed the form a big black
Brute and a great spell was casted over me, and I was
　　taken down to that place where
Fiends, warlocks, imps, beasts, satyrs, moved in fleshly
　　form: a wicked, most fantastic procession . . . goblins,
　　with faces of serpents, were there, vampires, cats and
　　one eyed owls, salamanders with bat wings and horrid
　　mouths swollen with blood . . . the pretty pink
　　bodies of babes died unbaptized,
　　pucks and pugs, naked legs, arms, bits of bodies,
　　drawn, skull-like heads, tortured eyes . . .
This is hell, I cried! And came awake trembling,
　　sweating, finding sundry things had been perpetrated
　　upon my flesh and within my body.

It has been said God sometimes chastises a whole nation
For sins of its most wicked citizen

I say it is loneliness that drives a person
        to seek companionhood with demons
A woman who accepts an infernal lover may not again content
        herself with the ruck of socially approved men
The same may be said of a man who has known nymphs, elves
        and witches
Will long for them again and again
Eschewing the feeble impuissant arms of artifact females
Society has a need to stigmatize
An individual in whom the
Greatness, guilt and sins of an entire nation may be
Projected
If witches did not exist men would create them —
The body of the child who has been sat upon as well as the body
Of the one who has been accused
        will be examined by the Most Holy
Reverend Cotton Mather.

Wherefore, I cry out upon the names
        written in the Black Book and those who have fornicated
        in the Divil's Din,
Cry out upon those who suckle with dogs, snakes and
        monkeys; those who seduced the good man and seduced the
        chaste woman, and those who have set upon my body
        and deranged my spirit and pinched me, hurting my flesh,
        and those who came to me in the dark opposite of the
        innocent person —
For mine eyes are blind, and cannot see.

I give you their names, and point them out
I will quake and quiver when their presence
        is upon me —
Spartacus is a witch! Joan of Arc is a witch! Galileo is
        a witch! Harriet Tubman, Gloria Richardson, Lillian
        Smith are witches! Hawthorne, Poe, Blake, Hart Crane,

Are witches! And the one called "Jesus" is definitely a witch!
Medgar Evers is a witch! Richard Wright is a witch!
Allen Ginsberg, Ishmael Reed, Karl Marx, are witches!
Jack Palance is a witch!
Mary Bethune, collecting walking cains of dead men, is
      a black witch!
And the duskman of black, spewing death ink into white eyes,
      is the Master of all darkness!
And you, Good woman Susanna!
      All are witches, coming out of the din of the devil,
      mating with themselves, opposing and victimizing,
      consorting with the outcast,
      walking and talking of unholy things —
Oh! — there is no good on earth, and sin is but a name
It is strange to see that the so-called good shrank not from
      the wicked, nor were the sinner abashed by the saints . . .
I am blind, and cannot see.

Wherefore, it is written that a witch shall not be suffered
      to live.
And, wherefore the most Holy Cotton Mather has, upon repeated instances
      and with reverence and much skill (at these things), examined the
      accused as well as the child who has been afflicted
And upon the accused, said Sarah Good and Goodwoman Susanna
      FOUND
A preternatural excrescence of flesh near the vagina which,
      upon various occasions of repeated and painful examination by the
      Most Holy Cotton Mather — FOUND
Such preternatural excrescence of flesh to fluctuate in size,
      color, and palpitation to stimulation;
And upon the child who was afflicted, said Abigail Moonlight,
      FOUND
Her in fits and, more than three times, hollowing like a
Jackal in the moon and rolling upon her bed in a most vulgar
      and unholy movement, and did, at last ascertain, said afflicted
      being a mere nine years old was big with Baby —

Oh! Such wickedness! Such sorcery! Could have been performed only
    by Asmodeus himself, or by an immaculate personage
    whose shape and form Asmodeus did assume —

And whereby, one of the accused, said Sarah Good, did confess
To such acts of witch craft and did cry out for
    mercy and repentance,
The second accused declares against all evidence, both spectral and
    objective, her innocence,
    and will not cry out for mercy or repentance!

It is written that a witch shall not be suffered to live
That without the awful presence of devils
Who among us may be certain of God —

Abigail Moonlight! Stand up and face your accusers!
I bring you a lantern!
Follow me. For you are blind
    and cannot see,
The evil in the world is man-made, and man must unmake it!
Take up this lantern, Abigail,
And follow.

   *   *   *

Litany in Winter's Garden

For Richard Wright

I

Unreal city
In the green fog of a winter Paris
Pagan, black magic light shimmering
In the night —
Fear death by the hand of a stranger.

The brown leaves lie crisp over winter Paris
The brown leaves are old hands, parched and wrinkled
The leaves are pages torn from a certain book,
Long forgotten,
Confiscated from your self in the dark place,
The leaves are faces of Negroes battered and beaten,
Flung down resounding against the metallic
Asphalt, the cold, dead asphalt.

I saw several men standing around a rock
Fear death.

II

It is winter here too, estranged one.
There is an army camp near by
This city belongs to the young men in brown,
The color of dead leaves.
It is winter now, and cold outside.
The soldiers will kill. They have been trained
To kill. They will shoot guns and drop bombs.
The leaves are brown and cover the ground
Like lips twisted and frail that once
Kissed dollar bills.
When the soldiers evacuate the city
The young women will be old.

Unreal city,
Fertile earth buried beneath the leaves of graveyards,
Mist hanging over, heavy fog, music from a distance —
Fear death at the end of an umbilical rope.

III

Father, Father in Heaven, why hast thou
Forsaken us? The labor unions are all corrupted.

The human heart, the twisted mouth and skeleton hands.
Blood on the leaves,
Death in the land.
Nude bodies hanging on twisted sticks.
There is blood on the totem pole of the western world.

Father, in thy house are many mansions,
In thy mouth is a tooth of solid, shimmering gold.
Father in Thy mansion you have buttressed many
Houses. Your daughters stand in
Doorways, the war has left us cold —
And colder yet, the tree of hope is bare,
Thy leaves are now brown on the ground,
Shapes of rust,
Shapes of dust to be blown away when the last
Truth is whispered.

The war has left us cold. The hot steal of hatred
Leaves us colder. And colder yet shall be our graves.
Give us love, Jesus, Savior O pilot us over!

Amen.
Amen.
Amen.

IV

Now there are no roses which might bloom.
Now there is no chalice from which to drink.
No wine that flows from heart to heart.
This garden is barren,
The evening has pulled down its shades —
Only the leaves, brown, crisp, and somehow, tender,
like the hands of someone
We love. Only
The leaves.

Fear death. Fire and water.
Death in a golden electric chair.
Fear hate in disguises —
An institution, a church, a government,
A shark-skin rain coat, a book,
Walking, smiling —
Bare headed,
Fear hate!

The soldiers kill. The government imprisons.
We must dispossess the hate merchants,
And let them run free, like blind Judases.
Or Baptists who have suddenly in the light been suddenly
Castrated by their own crimes.

V

Our language will tell on us.
At night with the lifting of the masks
And the disrobing — we lie down alone,
Without faces, without bodies.
I see hosts of people.
Our language will tell on us.

Countee Cullen died at the age of thirty.
Life sent him a rejection slip.

I see a group of efficient machines
Standing in the West.

VI

Father, why has thou forsaken us?
Why Father, on earth, in this garden, this vineyard of
The west, where autumn falls,
Why hast thou tolerated the erection of a totem pole,

Cast iron and gold, in the space where Thy son
Shed his blood?

Oh, Take the face of Jesus down
Take her wounded body and place it in a tomb

I see crowds of people throwing
Palms on the ground

VII

Unreal city.
Fear death when autumn, the strangler, comes —
Unreal city,
Autumn in the garden.
Leaves of my father's hand, and of his
Father who picked cotton, in the scorching fields
Of Alabama.

I shall place this hand, brown with clay and
muddy earth, that with which God fashioned man
And fashioned women —
I shall place it gently
Be reverent, thankful for this blood, pressed
From these leaves brown and falling, that by which
Your taking, the Flesh is healed.

Oh bright and morning star!
Oh silent powers that have seldom spoken!
Oh fallen leaves, Oh brown crisp hands of god!
Touch the love mouldering in our hearts
And against that touch let no words be spoken.

The Passengers

For Allen Ginsberg

Once dawn
A silent train pulled into the station of America,
Ghostly, invisible, no one saw it, no one heard its
    grinding wheels come to a stop.

Out of the train the passengers came like mummies, silent,
    sleepy-eyed, moving in and among the people
    like zombies from some dark mysterious place in the universe
But they are not mummies, they are not dead.

These are the passengers going to and fro among the cities,
Walking up and down, milling around, sitting in on important
    conferences, looking, watching, hearing, peering around,
    observing, slipping into hallways, riding on elevators
    visiting fan meetings, attending football games, sitting
    among movie-goers, taking notes at the U.N., standing
    amid crowds, at street corner speeches, coming up and
    down escalators in the Pan Am building, going here and there
    riding subways, buses, air planes, walking the streets,
    commuting from town to city, walking among riots and public
    commotions, standing in lines, eating in restaurants,
    witnessing plots, robberies, deaths, conspiracies, lovers
    making love, keeping records, filing away papers, money,
    keeping statistics on everything, the birth rate and the
    death rate, growth of cities, decline of rural areas,
    watching unmindful people walking under umbrellas when
    it is no longer raining!

Silently, solemnly, the passengers are among us, coming and
    going, standing, looking, counting, taking down names, adding,
    multiplying, dividing, subtracting,
Everywhere they are among us, in sleep and waking,

And nobody hears them, nobody sees them —
Except one!

And he is frightened by their ghostly manner, intrigued and
    excited by their mysterious demeanor, enthralled and electrified by
    their whispering and going to and fro in the manner of
    sleepwalkers, incensed by their enigma;
But they are not mysterious, they have no enigma.
And the one runs among them shouting from the depths of his
    bowels, haranguing, imploring, nudging, pinching,
    kicking, screaming...
But the passengers will not be interrupted, will not bring color
    and visibility to their presence or to their forms;
    they remain unseen, unheard, solemn, stealthy, invisible;
Ghostly, like zombies, they move as if to an unheard music in
    their minds,
Back into the waiting invisible train standing in the
    station of America like a suspended dirge —
And they take their seats.

But the train does not move, the wheels refuse to grind, the
    Steam will not explode, the piston won't gyrate;
As if propelled by a compulsion beneath the blood or by a
    commitment sealed in a vault too imperative for denial,
Stern-faced, silent, solemn, the passengers ride in unison
    and empty out into the cities again,
Going about their awful business, taking down names, writing in notebooks,
    books of red, blue, green, spots of orange and hectic
    colors, looking at billboards, pee-peeing like average men and women
    and like big names in high and low echelons of politics, society, economics,
    or like just plain pee-peeing people, in subway stations, at bus stops,
    behind parked cars, in dark alleys of crowded restrooms. Pee-peeing in
      locker rooms,
    invisible, talking to no one, being seen, heard,
    felt by no one, going to and fro, private houses cleaning,
    sitting at tables, getting in and out of taxicabs, solemn, serene,

in groups of threes and fours, pulling cups from cup dispensaries,
    going alone at lunch counters, with multitudes, silent, unobserved,
    taking coffee breaks with millions throughout the teeming cities,
    standing at the racetracks, observing what the police are doing, watching
        the habits of
    birds, keeping tab on the weather, cleaning up scraps, washing,
    ironing, clearing away old clothes, debris, empty beer cans,
    and abandoned love affairs, fanning away the smoke of the immaculate
    mushroom —
Mixing with communists, black niggers, white bigots,
    liberals, extremists and reactionaries alike,
    mingling, aggregating, jitterbugging
    among dykes, faggots, pimps, riders,
    poets, painters, negro prostitutes.

They are preparing, secretly, solemnly preparing for the spinal screams,
    the jerking and throbbing of the sphincters, the clinging and
    clawing on the back, the slow, involuntary tears, the
    sighs and spontaneous utterances of pain and ecstasy;
    They are getting ready for the Womb of Woman when she
    comes for the third and final time.

❊ ❊ ❊

Wooing of the Little Girl Who Lives in a Dark Hall

To Ree Dragonette

Leap upon your mouth fire.
Fig leaves leap. Birdtongue.
Pegasus sealed
In the winged iron of the great birthhouse.
Childhood is a time for searching
And a time for hiding.

Go on to cross legs and forked sticks.
Crucifix of thighbeam.

Backward, forward;
Dragon night ride hot heifer on the mind.
Womanhood is a place to be young in
To rebel, to be a fool in.

O weep lone little girl
In the naked hallway!
Do not be frightened of hands.
Pain is a harp for wind and voice
For voice and rain
And one mystic memory contained in
The marrow tickling.

O come out of the dark hallway
Little girl child.
See, where the great bull lights
Across the sky, sundown
Is no longer there.
See to the left the sign of the scorpion
See to the right the vector of the v-bone.

O come out of the dark hallway
Little girl child
Let leap fig leaves from your breasts.
Let your mouth leap fire.

Splendid spread.
Sound
Elemental ecstasy.

Mad Dogs in Vietnam

Mad dogs gone mad in Vietnam
Snarling from behind barricades of fear
Pouncing upon every sound they hear
Mad dogs gone mad in Vietnam.

In the great White House of the United States
The mad dog of mad dogs devours a bloody steak —
The blood is the blood of madness and hate
The steak is the flesh of innocent people
Murdered in the streets,
And the mad dog licks his chops and goes to sleep.

Killing for the madness of killing!
Kill the old, the young, the unwilling
Killing in the name of Democracy
Kill all the dirty colored people but don't kill me!

Kill the babies sucking their mother's tits
Kill them and apologize!
Shoot them, bomb them, blast them to bits
Kill them and Rationalize!
Kill them in Vietnam or Birmingham
Kill them in the name of God Damn!

Mad dogs done god mad in Vietnam
Snarling from behind barricades of lies
Seeing themselves in the dead people's eyes
Mad dogs done gone mad in Vietnam!

A Canticle for the 1960s

For Ree Dragonette, in memorial

Haight Ashbury
I say Haight Ashbury

Haight Ashbury,
I say Haight Ashbury
Selma Alabama,
I say Selma Alabama,

Jacksonville, Chicago, Birmingham,
Soledad, San Quentin.

University of California at Berkeley
University of California at San Jose
University of California at Sacramento,
Marcuse, Frantz Fanon, Reggie Debray,
C. Wright Mills and Che Guevara, a funeral
For Medgar Evers, for Nkrumah, Richard Wright,
Funeral for Eric Dolphy, Charles Olson, Bobby
Hutton and Patrice Lumumba.

I say Haight Ashbury
I say uptown in Harlem
I say Speakers Corner at 125th Street and 7th Ave
I say Times Square
I say Downtown on the Lower Eastside
Avenue "A" Avenue "B" Avenue "C" Avenue "D" —
Exhume the life and blood of New York City.

I say March on Washington
I say Flower Power
I say Black Power
I say Viet Nam, Black Panther, Black Studies,
      Reverend Moon and Gay Liberation

I say I saw it at Woodstock
I heard it in Slugs, I heard it at Max's Kansas City,
I heard it at the Band Box
I heard it at the Five Spot and I heard it at the Gate
That fronts the gravel pavilion leading
To Léopold Senghor's state house and
To Malcolm X's grave.

I say Turn on! Tune in! Drop out!
Oh yes, Turn on! Tune in! Drop Out!
Burn baby burn!
I say "Blow Up," I say "Z," I say "Easy Rider,"
Haight Ashbury
Hate Jerry Rubin
Hate your mother's false teeth
Hate your great white father's false underwear

I say Selma Alabama, I say Attica,
I say Freedom Ride, I say Wade-In, I say Sit-In,
I say Jackson State University,
Kent State University, Folsom Prison, Watts Los Angeles,
Turn on! Tune in! Drop out! Burn baby burn!
I say Black is Beautiful! I say People are Beautiful!
I say Hippies, Runaways, Yippies and Jaybirds
Let em riot, let em freak, let trip, let em get blown away!
I say homicide, genocide
Murdered in motels and motorcades, murdered in Algiers,
Dying in model cities of Cleveland, Dayton, Detroit.

I say rise up on your toes, extend your limbs, reach your
    arms and hands up to the sky
And sing a praise for the 1960's.

Joy you gonna see
Joy you gonna see
Joy for the dead

And joy for the living —
Alive Richie Havens!
Alive Marianne Faithful, Peter Townshend, Eric Clapton,
    Bob Dylan, Joan Baez!
Alive James Baldwin!
Alive Steve Cannon!
Alive Ree Dragonette!
Alive Sun Ra!
Alive Cecil Taylor!
Alive Ed Sanders, Ishmael Reed, Ann Guilfoyle,
Alive Muhammad Ali!
And alive Michael Horowitz, Adrian Mitchell, Jeff
    Nuttall, Ted Joans and Brother Antoninus!
Alive Jimi Hendrix!
Alive Janis Joplin!
Alive Ella Estell my grandmother!
Alive John Coltrane!
Alive is the Audubon Ballroom!
Alive is the mountain top!
Alive! Alive! alive!

Haight Ashbury
Hate Memphis Tennessee
Hate the guns that burst open your guts
    The bullets that burst your skull and settled your brains
    upon the wrought-iron balcony and on the birds
    nesting on the branches of the imported exotic palm trees
I say Haight Ashbury
Hate jitterbugging in the streets written on the wall
    above Verta Mae's fireplace
Fireplace where Sam Greenlee knee-bowed and body-bent
Sam Greenlee the spook who wept by the door in the
    Presbyterian Hospital across from the Audubon
    Ballroom at 168th Street and Upper Broadway —

Upper Broadway at 168th Street
Upper Broadway at 141st Street
Upper Broadway at l6lst Street
Upper Broadway at Columbus and 97th Street at the sliding
    steel of semi's rolling over the great slab
    across the majestic bleakness of Americana —

I say, the West Coast came from the East Coast
And the East Coast emanated out of the sea chasing its
    own blood across the magic carpet of red, white and blue,
    livid with murder of zero populations —
Que pasa, Amigo —
    Nada pasa
Que pasa Amiga —
    Nada pasa
Que pasa esta noche en el barrio?
Oh, Langston Hughes!
Oh, John Coltrane!
Oh, Richard Wright!
Oh, Eric Dolphy!
Oh, Patrice Lumumba!
Oh, Ree . . .
Resurrection!
Resurrection!
Resurrection to the fool on the hill!
Resurrection to Evinrude outboard motors
Resurrection to Stokely Carmichael invited to the West
    Coast where John J. Jasper stuck a gun in his mouth
    and pronounced him Minister of the Forms of Things
    Unknown
Of exiles in Cuba, China, Algiers,
Of ashes and experience.

Rap Brown rap down,
Bill Burroughs
Tangiers, Ibiza, Formentero,

I say Acapulco Gold
I say Afghanistan Black
Chairman Mao's red book
Ornette Coleman, John Paul Sartre, SDS,
Symbionese Liberation Army . . .
Archie Shepp, Miles Davis, Bertrand Russell,
Julian Beck and Judith Malina,
Lenny Bruce, Angela Davis,
Maryanne Raphael, Allen Ginsberg, Yevtushenko,
Lawrence Ferlinghetti, John Cage,
Congress on Racial Equality,
Southern Christian Leadership Conference,
Student Non-Violent Coordinating Committee,
Rallying at the New School for Social Research
Rallying at the Judson Church, at St. Marks in the Bowery;
Years of tears in retrospect, long shots that fell short;
East Village Other, City Lights, Les Deux Megots, Cafe WHA,
In and out of the Night Owl, Up and down Porto
Bello Road, all around Notting Hill Gate, up and down avenue "B"
In the Annex and Out of the Dom,
Robin Morgan writing in the Nickle Review, Tom McGrath writing
      in the International Times —
Times of instant replay —
Times of shucking and jiving —
Times of the Pentagon, the CIA, the state dept.,
      Shuttling back and forth through the Middle East,
      To Africa, to Europe, to Russia,
      Scars of genocide and hegemony —
Times of LSD riding on white horses —
Times of *Dutchman*, *Slaves* and *Toilets* —

Sing a song for Paul Blackburn!
I say sing a song for Paul Blackburn
Sing a song for the Old Reliable, for Carol Bergé
for Diane Wakoski, for Diane di Prima,
A song for women in prison —

A song for the bullet . . .
And sing a song for the Audubon Ballroom.

Because of the graves beneath the petrol fields in Biafra
Because of Susan Sherman
Because of Howard Ant
Because of Marguerite Harris
Because of Joe Overstreet
Because of Number 44 Baker Street
Because of Kate Millet and "The Second Sex"
Because of Claude Brown and John A. Williams
Because of Jomo Kenyatta,
Because of Daffodils and Lilac,
Because of crimes of passion in California and Cambodia,
Because of the Cedar Bar on University Place
Because of Washington Square Park
Because of Hyde Park
Because of Central Park
Because of Vanessa Redgrave
Because of Jane Fonda
Because of Germaine Greer and the Female Eunuch
Because of R. D. Laing and the Dialectics of Liberation
Because of the Ambiance, and the Q Club and Because of Bow
    Road and Bow Chapel and Brick Lane and White Chapel and
    Mothersill and Swish Cheese and Charing Cross and
    Trafalgar Square and West Indians and East
    Asians and Pakistanis and poor whites of kin,
Because of the red call box and tobacconist shop and five
    roads intersecting at Farringdon and Roseberry Avenue
Where the largest sorting post office exists in the world —
Because of "I have a dream"
Because of "I'm black and I'm proud"
Because of the Bay of Pigs
Because of "Beatle Mania"
Because of "Right on, Brother"
Because of the Jimi Hendrix Experience

Because of Androgenous loud speakers —
I say rise up on all fours, cast your eyes to the clouds
And sing a praise for the 60's
And sing a song for assassins, a song for Jack Ruby
    and Sirhan Bishara Sirhan, and for the assassin
    of the man who cried "I Am!"

Said, Haight Ashbury
Said, Selma Alabama
I said, sing a praise for Doctor William Carlos Williams,
For Doctor Black Mountain School of Poetics
Doctor Tommie Smith
Doctor John Carlos
Doctor Jayne Cortez
Doctor Wole Soyinka

Said, rise upon your feet and sing a praise to Kathleen
    Cleaver, Angela Davis, Sonia Sanchez, Nikki Giovanni,
    June Jordan, Alice Walker, a praise to Robin Morgan
    Writing in the Nickle Review —

Say a praise for Ram John Holder, For George Lamming, for C. L. R.
    James, for Bloke Modisane and for the Mangrove,
    but especially for Bloke Modisane
    who fled from Babylon to Babylon —
Sing a song of praise, and do not mourn.

    (1979)

Chronology

1932   April 28: Calvin Coolidge Hernton born to Magnolia Jackson in Chattanooga, Tennessee. Raised by grandmother, Ella Estell — "my first and deepest influence, mentor, and teacher" — for the first sixteen years of his life in Chattanooga and Tullahoma. Hernton later recalls growing up during the era of the Great Depression, Jim Crow, the Scottsboro Boys Case, and the Second World War in his essay "Chattanooga Black Boy" (1996). Works as a delivery boy, a shoe-shine boy, a pinsetter, and at a steel erection and plumbing supply plant.

1950   Awarded an academic scholarship to attend HBCU Talladega College, whose interracial faculty and radical scholars earned it the nickname "the backdoor to the Kremlin." Nicknamed "Socrates" for his serious scholarly bent and reservoir of knowledge and wisdom, Hernton's friends include the parents of poet Harryette Mullen. Teachers include the Marxist Fritz Pappenheim, who encourages Hernton to apply for a Fulbright Scholarship; Pappenheim is expelled from the college for his politics in 1952. Hernton will dedicate his book *White Papers for White Americans* to Pappenheim.

1954   Graduates from Talladega. Writes his earliest poems: "Remigrant" appears in *Phylon*.

1955–56   Studies at Fisk University on a Fulbright Scholarship; earns a master's degree in sociology with a thesis entitled "A Thematic Analysis of Editorials and Letters to the Editors Regarding the Montgomery Bus Protest Movement." Has a six-hour meeting with Lillian Smith, author of *Killers of the Dream* (1949), whose study of the "psychosexual profit system" in the American South is an influence on his own *Sex and Racism in America*. Along with Ella Estell, Smith is the dedicatee of Hernton's *The Coming of Chronos to the House of Nightsong* (1964). Member of workshop led by Robert Hayden, a friend and mentor. While at Fisk, surveilled by the FBI on the basis of early poems.

1956–57 Briefly based in New York. Reads with poet Raymond R. Patterson in a series curated by Patterson in June, 1957. Associates with Langston Hughes.

1957–61 Teaches social science at four HBCUs: Benedict College (1957–58), Alabama A&M (1958–59), Edward Waters College (1959–60), and Southern University and A&M (1960–61).

1958 Marries Mildred Webster, a Talladega classmate. They have one son, Antone. Poems appear in European anthologies edited by Eric Walrond and Rosey E. Pool.

1961 Moves to New York to study Sociology at Columbia University (1961). Works for the Department of Welfare (1961–62) and National Opinion Research Center (1963–64).

1962 Poems appear in European anthologies: Rosey Pool's *Beyond the Blues* and Paul Breman's *Sixes and Sevens*. Summer: Umbra Poets Workshop founded by Tom Dent. Hernton, Dent, and Henderson are co-editors of the group's magazine.

1963 During this period, reads at Café Le Metro, Les Deux Megots, and other venues associated with the Lower East Side arts scene. Develops close friendships and artistic relationships with Ishmael Reed, David Henderson, and Ree Dragonette, among many others. Hernton recalls this period in the essays "Umbra: A Personal Recounting" (1993) and "Les Deux Megots Mon Amour" (1985). Attends the March on Washington in August, the subject of an essay in *White Papers for White Americans*.

1964 Hernton's work included in Langston Hughes's anthology *New Negro Poets: U.S.A.* Publishes *The Coming of Chronos to the House of Nightsong* with Interim Books. December: reads "The Gift Outraged" at Columbia University alongside Allen Ginsberg. Appears in Aldo Tambellini's installation *Black Zero*.

1965 April: Participates in reading sponsored by the Harlem Writers Guild at the New School. Participates in the Black Arts Repertory Theater/School (BARTS) in Harlem, reading his poetry and directing a production of Charles Patterson's play *Black Ice*. Hernton's sociological study, *Sex and Racism in America*, is published by Doubleday. Departs for London (UK) in the summer with poet John Keys and psychiatrist Joseph Berke, having received a fellowship to study at the Institute of Phenomenological Studies directed by R. D. Laing at Kingsley Hall. Begins work on the novel *Scarecrow*.

1966	Involved with the Caribbean Artists Movement (CAM), newly founded by Andrew Salkey, John La Rose, and Edward Kamau Brathwaite. *White Papers for White Americans*, a book of essays, is published in America by Doubleday. Publishes in English socialist journal *Peace News*.
1967	Spends time in Lund, Sweden.
1968	On the faculty for the Antiuniversity of London, a short-lived radical educational experiment at 49 Rivington Street, Shoreditch, and founded in February 1968 by a group including anti-psychiatrists R. D. Laing and David Cooper, feminist scholar Juliet Mitchell, and cultural studies pioneer Stuart Hall. Lasting until August, the Antiuniversity has around three hundred students and fifty faculty, and ties to the International Free University Movement, including the Free University of New York and the New Experimental College in Denmark. Other lecturers include Obi Egbuna, Allen Ginsberg, and Stokely Carmichael. Hernton's work, including the lengthy essay "Dynamite Growing Out of Their Skulls!" appears in Amiri Baraka and Larry Neal's collection *Black Fire: An Anthology of Afro-American Writing*.
1969	Appears in Clarence Major's anthology *The New Black Poetry*.
1970	Returns to the United States to take up a position as poet-in-residence at Central State University.
1971	Appointed writer-in-residence at Oberlin College. *Coming Together: Black Power, White Hatred, and Sexual Hang-Ups* published by Random House.
1972	Appointed Associate Professor in Oberlin's newly-founded Black Studies Department. Students include actor Avery Brooks, for whose television show, *A Man Called Hawk*, Hernton later serves as scriptwriter and consultant.
1973	Appears in Paul Breman's anthology *You Better Believe It*, published by Penguin Books.
1974	*Scarecrow* published by Doubleday; *The Cannabis Experience: An Interpretive Study of the Effects of Marijuana and Hashish*, the first sociological study on the effects of cannabis use, co-authored with Joseph Berke, published in England by Peter Owen.
1975	Divorced from Mildred (Webster) Hernton.
1976	*Medicine Man: Collected Poems* published by Reed, Cannon & Johnson, with a preface by Joe Johnson.

1980	Named Professor of African American Studies and Creative Writing at Oberlin. Increasingly engaged in pedagogy and in feminist scholarship — or as he prefers to name it, "anti-sexist" — scholarship. Continues to teach and publish in academic journals.
1987	Publishes the literary study *The Sexual Mountain and Black Women Writers: Adventures in Sex, Literature, and Real Life*, dedicated to the memory of poet Sarah Webster Fabio.
1990	Writes introductions to the *Collected Stories of Chester Himes* and to a reprint of *Muntu* by Janheinz Jahn.
1997	Appointed chair of African American Studies at Oberlin.
1998	Marries Mary O'Callaghan.
1999	Retires from Oberlin College. Final book, *The Red Crab Gang and Black River Poems*, published by Ishmael Reed Publishing Company.
2000	December: Visits Cuba for a reading organized by Margaret Porter and Quincy Troupe's VeVe Art and Performance Gallery. Reads his poems in Spanish translation, including "The Distant Drum."
2001	Dies in his home in Oberlin on September 30th after a long battle with cancer.

Notes to the Poems

Publication information, revision history, and additional information is provided below. Poems that appear in *Medicine Man: Collected Poems* (Reed, Cannon & Johnson, 1976) often contain minor variations from their original printings in magazines, anthologies, and other venues; in most cases we have treated the *Medicine Man* printing as definitive, unless otherwise indicated.

ABBREVIATIONS

MM   *Medicine Man: Collected Poems* (Berkeley, CA: Reed, Cannon & Johnson, 1976).

OUL   Calvin C. Hernton Collection, MSS14, Ohio University Libraries, Mahn Center for Archives and Special Collections.

RPP   Rosey Pool Papers, TS 17/19 (verse), Folder H, Calvin Hernton, University of Sussex Special Collections.

NOTES FOR SOUTH TO NORTH: EARLY WORK

Statement

First published in *Sixes and Sevens: An Anthology of New Poems*, ed. Paul Breman (London: Paul Breman, 1962).

Remigrant

First printed in *Phylon* 15, no. 1 (1st Qtr., 1954): 89. Reprinted in *Sixes and Sevens*. Revised and reprinted in *MM*. Stanza 1: For "capable," *Sixes and Sevens* reads "qualified"; for "All men, free men, almost.": "All men, almost equal men, free men." Stanza 2: For "As a human being, / As a Black man.": "As a human being, as an / Equal man."

The Underlying Strife

First printed in *Phylon* 16, no. 4 (4th Qtr., 1955): 462. Reprinted in *Mainstream* XVI, no. 7 (July 1963: "Umbra Poets" feature): 11–13, and in *MM*.

The Distant Drum

First printed in *Ik Zag Hoe Zwart Ik Was / I Saw How Black I Was: Poetry of North American Negroes: A Bilingual Anthology*, ed. Rosey E. Pool and Paul Breman (The Hague, Holland: Piet Bakker, 1958) and *Beyond the Blues*, ed. Rosey Pool (Lympne, Kent: Hand and Flowers Press, 1962); reprinted in

MM and numerous anthologies. Hernton's most anthologized poem, "The Distant Drum," was set to music by Hans Werner Henze in 1973 as part of the song-cycle *Voices*, alongside poems by others including Bertolt Brecht, Ho Chi Minh, Victor Hernández Cruz, Heinrich Heine, Welton Smith, and Dudley Randall. Recording available as Henze, *Voices* (Decca Records, HEAD 19/20, 1978).

For Ghana, 1957

Originally published as "West at Bay (For Ghana, 1957)" in *Sixes and Sevens*. Reprinted and revised in *MM*. Stanza 1: For "The hand who ravished a continent," *Sixes and Sevens* reads "The West lies across the map"; for "False gods are falling": "Fair gods are falling. / Shadows are rising." Stanza 2 opens with the deleted lines: "Yes, we are going to suffer now! / We are not going to shake hands and forget. / We are going to repent." In stanza 3, for "I see a sun falling back into the sea. / I see a moon going down in the west": "I see a light falling back into the sea. / I see a star going down in the West"; for "predatory bird": "good-luck bird."

Blues Spiritual

First published in *Sixes and Sevens*. Reprinted in *MM*.

Richard Wright

Two Versions. Version 1 from RPP. Version 2 published in *MM*. It's our supposition that the second poem condenses and revises the list of names in stanza 1 to create a new poem, and we've included the two poems side by side to suggest Hernton's revision process.

Being Exit in the World

First published as "A Being Exit in the World" in *Beyond the Blues*, ed. Rosey Pool (Hand and Flowers Press, 1962). Reprinted with variants in *Sixes and Sevens* and *MM*. Stanza 2: For "Man cycled and ethos lorned," *Beyond the Blues* reads "Cradle-weaned and love torn." Stanza 3: For "Void in the world I exist": "Black in the world I exist in it"; for "Alienated as at first": "And estranged as at first." In stanza 4, the original printing opens with the following lines:

Oh, take my tongue, America!
From the meshes of my mouth I give it.
Put it in your pocket,
Hang it on a pole and let it fly!

For "And Being exists me": "And being black exits me, assaults the flowing syrups"; for "My essence visits a million dark rooms / Pulsing, I lie naked with sleepers": "My essence visits naked rooms, / Pulsing, I lie and die with lovers." For the concluding lines, "It is my ecstasy, / I am the leper who suffers to be.": "And it is *my* anguish, / For I am the man who suffers to be God."

The Wall

First published in *Sixes and Sevens*. Reprinted in *MM*.

Feeling

First published in the *Pittsburgh Courier* (May 8, 1954). Reprinted in *MM*.

Blues for Handy

Included in materials sent to Rosey Pool for *Beyond the Blues* (RPP) but not printed therein. First printed in *Negro Digest* 69 (September 1964). Reprinted in *MM*. "Blues for Handy" is a single by Bill Doggett, released in 1957. The *MM* printing lists the italicized lines as titles, but the manuscript and first printing indicate them instead as choruses or refrains.

Young Negro Poet

Published in *Sixes and Sevens*, reprinted in *Mainstream* XVI, no. 7 (July 1963: "Umbra Poets" feature): 11–13, and in revised form as "Ballad of a Young Jacklegged Poet" in *MM*, where it opens the volume. We here include the earlier, rather than the revised version; it was this earlier version that Robert Hayden encountered and praised (as Hernton mentions in the 1981 essay-memoir "The Passion of Robert Hayden"), which appeared in the Umbra poets feature of *Mainstream* and in the Hayden anthology *Kaleidoscope*. The revisions in *MM* are primarily adjustments to punctuation and mise-en-page, and the substitution of "jacklegged" for "negro" in all cases.

NOTES FOR THE LOWER EAST SIDE AND UMBRA

Umbra: A Personal Recounting

First published in *African American Review* 27, no. 4 (Winter 1993: "Lower East Side" feature): 579–84. Uncollected.

Ballad of the Shoe String Kid

First published in *MM*. Stanza 3: "the quarter of the blacks" echoes Henderson's "Black is the Home," printed in *Umbra*'s first issue. "West lost" alludes to the 1962 blockbuster Western *How the West Was Won*, dirs. Henry Hathaway, John Ford, and George Marshall. In Stanza 9, "Ask your mother": Continuing to play the dozens with Henderson here, Hernton invokes the title to Langston Hughes's 1961 collection *Ask Your Mama: 12 Moods for Jazz*, a significant influence on Henderson. The Hughes reference is picked up in Stanza 10, where "the burnt dream deferred" alludes to Hughes's classic "Harlem."

The Long Blues; 125th Street, Harlem, U.S.A.; Street Scene
> First published in *Umbra* I (Winter 1963). Reprinted in *MM*. "125th Street" first published as "125th Street (Harlem, New York)." In the final stanza, where *MM* has "Upon my brow the mark of Ham," the *Umbra* printing reads "Upon my brow the mark of Idiom." OUL contains an unpublished variant of "Street Scene," retitled "Soho," replacing "Go to Hell, sonofabitch!" with "Fuck off, black bastard!"

Burnt Sabbath, Mount Morris Park, Harlem
> First printed in *MM*.

Hate Poem
> First printed in *Umbra* 5: Latin / Soul feature (1975): 85. The poem was performed as part of Aldo Tambellini's multi-media piece *Black Zero* in 1965. Uncollected.

Elements of Grammar
> First published in *The New Black Poetry*, ed/ Clarence Major (New York: International Publishers, 1969). Reprinted in *MM*. In the OUL manuscript, the dedication "To Little John" reads "John Little." We have been unable to definitively identify who is meant here. One possibility is that "Little John" or "John Little" may be a pun on the name of Hernton's friend John Keys, with whom he traveled to England in 1965. In "Umbra: A Personal Recounting," Hernton calls this "a famous Lower East Side poem," written for and performed at a reading at the New School for Social Research — likely part of the reading series at the New School sponsored by the Harlem Writers Guild in April 1965, which featured Hernton, Amiri Baraka, and others.

The Gift Outraged
> First published in *Fire*, no. 2 (March 1968). Reprinted in *MM*. In "Umbra: A Personal Recounting," Hernton notes reading this poem "hot-off-the-typewriter" at a Columbia University reading, which took place in December 1964. (See also Alan Feldman, "Poetry of the Body," *Columbia Daily Spectator* CIX, no. 44 (December 1964): 3.

NOTES FOR THE COMING OF CHRONOS
TO THE HOUSE OF NIGHTSONG

Les Deux Megots Mon Amour" (1985)
> Published in *Light Years: An Anthology on Sociocultural Happenings (Multimedia in the East Village, 1960–1966)*, ed. Carol Bergé (New York: Spuyten Duyvil, 2010): 291–308.

The Coming of Chronos to the House of Nightsong
 Published as a pamphlet by Interim Books in 1964, with illustrations by
 John Fawcett. Excerpts also appear in *You Better Believe It*, ed. Paul Breman
 (London: Penguin, 1972). This is the first complete republication of the
 poem.

NOTES FOR MEDICINE MAN
Medicine Man
 First printed as the title poem to *MM*, but likely written earlier. In a report
 on a reading given by Umbra poets to launch the BARTS, Clayton Riley
 notes: "[Hernton's] verse recollection of a trip to his former S. Carolina
 home was, in anguished intensity, a work of eminent beauty." Though he
 does not give the poem's title, the description strongly suggests that it may
 have been "Medicine Man," in which case it may have been written by 1965.
 There are further textual clues: the poem's line "Thirty red years contending
 with Satan" and its references to April, the month of Hernton's birth, suggest
 that it may have been written in his thirtieth year, in 1962.
Almost Sunday
 First printed in *MM*. The opening line, "From Gany Mede to cat of
 mountain," likely puns both on Ganymede, the Trojan youth who, in
 Homer's account, was kidnapped to serve as Zeus's cupbearer on Olympus,
 and on the Medes, an ancient Iranian group who occupied mountainous
 regions of Iran in the eighth and seventh centuries BC.
Taurus by Aster Fire
 Dedication: "To Ree Dragonette." First published in *MM*. In "Les Deux
 Megots Mon Amor," Hernton notes this poem as a response to Dragonette's
 "Buffalo Waits in the Cave of Dragons" in *Umbra*, no. 2 (December 1963):
 46–49, and subsequently collected in Dragonette's collection *Parable of the
 Fixed Stars* (New York: Allograph Books, 1968).
A Ballad of the Life and Times of Joe Louis, The Great Brown Bomber
 First printed in *MM*. The first line of Section VI indicates that the poem was
 written in 1971.
The Patient: Rockland County Sanitarium
 Section I was first printed as a separate poem entitled "Madhouse" in *New
 Negro Poets: U.S.A.*, ed. Langston Hughes (Bloomington: Indiana University
 Press, 1964): 101–2, and it has been anthologized under that name. The full
 poem was first printed in *The Poetry of Black America: Anthology of the 20th
 Century*, ed. Arnold Adoff (New York: Harper & Row, 1973) and reprinted in

MM. With the exception of the first two lines and the final line of the stanza, the majority of Section III, stanza 2 appears in early drafts of the novel *Scarecrow*, published in *19 Necromancers from Now* ed. Ishmael Reed (Garden City, New York: Doubleday, 1970).

In a text written for "A Program of Poetry" at Alabama A&M College on November 24, 1953, Hernton offers the following comment on the "Madhouse" versions of the poem:

> Now some people have funny notions about writers and poets, especially Negro writers and poets. They think if you are a Negro, well you ought to write about race, usually the race problem. And if you don't you are not an artist. Now many critics and mostly all white folks think this, and this doesn't bother me at all — I know they are prejudiced. When I hear Negroes saying the same thing, I am surprised. They criticize Frank Yerby and Willard Motley on this account, and many whites really do not know that Frank Yerby is a Negro. Frank Yerby writes historical stories about the white plantation South, and he is a great artist and a master storyteller. Richard Wright writes about the race problem, and he is a great artist and a master storyteller. James Baldwin, in *Giovanni's Room*, writes about a powerful love triangle in Paris between two men and a woman whose races are not mentioned, and that book is a sublime work of art in the English language. The point I'm trying to make is: an artist is not an artist according to *what* he writes about or what race he belongs to! What makes an artist an artist is analogous to what makes a scientist a scientist. He may be a biologist, a chemist, a psychiatrist, a sociologist, a physicist, a Jew, a Chinese, a German — what makes him a scientist is not his particular field or his race, but his pursuit of Truth according to the principles of a definite method. What makes an artist is not his race or the particular thing he writes about, whether love, or war, or nature — but the fact that he takes what he thinks and feels is Truth and renders it up in a way that is emotionally dignified and beautiful!
>
> So: I don't write about love, or the trees and the sunset, or the race problem all of the time. Sometimes, most of the times, I write about the experience of life itself! [...] This is a poem about life itself. (OUL, Box 2, Folder 7).

Scarecrow

First published in *MM*.

Fall Down
> First published in *Dices or Black Bones: Black Voices of the Seventies*, ed. Adam
> David Miller (Boston, MA: Houghton Mifflin Co., 1970). Reprinted in *MM*
> and in numerous anthologies. Eric Dolphy died in 1964.

D Blues
> First published in *The Poetry of Black America: Anthology of the 20th Century*,
> ed. Arnold Adoff (New York: Harper & Row, 1973). Reprinted in *MM*.

NOTES FOR RIOTS AND REVOLUTIONS

Dynamite Growing Out of Their Skulls
> Appeared in *Black Fire: An Anthology of Afro-American Writing*, ed. Amiri
> Baraka and Larry Neal (New York: William Morrow, 1968). Uncollected.

Terrorist
> First published in *Liberator* 5, no. 5 (May 1965) and the *Carleton Miscellany*
> (Winter 1965). Reprinted in *MM*.

The Mob
> First published in *MM*.

Jitterbugging in the Streets
> Published in *Streets* 1, no. 2 (May–June, 1965). *Streets* was a New Left
> magazine edited by Paul Jasper, Mario Riofrancos, and Stefan Uhse. This
> issue also features Amiri Baraka's "Three Movements and a Coda," alongside
> Jean-Paul Sartre and Frantz Fanon. Hernton mentions this publication
> in "Umbra: A Personal Recounting" and the way that the poem "spread
> around the neighborhood." Notable reprintings include in "Poets of the
> Insurrections," in *American Dialog* 4, no. 2 (Autumn 1967): 12–13; in the
> booklet to *New Jazz Poets* (1967), on which Hernton reads the poem; and
> in *Black Fire*. Revised and included in *MM*. In the final line of penultimate
> stanza, "Marques Haynes is a globetrotting basketball playing fool" refers
> to a basketball player with the Harlem Globetrotters. After quitting the
> Globetrotters in 1953, Haynes started his own team, the Fabulous Magicians,
> sponsored by Schaefer Brewing Company. See A. S. (Doc) Young,
> "Basketball's Black Entrepreneur," *Ebony* (Mar 1971): 96–103.

NOTES FOR "WITHOUT A PASSPORT TO HUMANITY":
LONDON POEMS

An Unexpurgated Communiqué to David Henderson
> First printed in *Umbra Anthology* (1967–1968): 19–24. Reprinted with

revisions in *MM*. We follow the reprint in every instance apart from the final three lines, where *MM* substitutes: "Every night I get stoned in the Seven Stars / And dream the dream of jungles." Section 3, line 2: "It is alright to drill a hole in your skull and avant-garde / into childfoolery and senility" is a reference to the infamous "trepanning" experiments of British heiress Amanda Feilding, documented in the film *Heartbeat in the Brain*.

Game Life, London 1967
Evergreen Review 13, no. 63 (February 1969). Reprinted in *MM*.

Country
Resurgence 2, no. 12 / *New Departures* 5 (Spring 1970), a joint issue of poetry magazine *New Departures* and "Fourth World" peace movement magazine *Resurgence*. Uncollected.

NOTES FOR OBERLIN, OHIO: LATER WORK

Chattanooga Black Boy
Appeared in *Names We Call Home: Autobiography on Racial Identity*, eds. Becky Thompson and Sangeeta Tyagi (London and New York: Routledge, 1996). Uncollected.

Low Down and Sweet
First printed in *Yardbird Reader* 1 (1972): 127–29. Reprinted in *MM*.

Hands
In *Black American Literature Forum* 14, no. 3 (Autumn 1980: "Umbra Poets" feature, edited by Tom Dent). Uncollected.

Rites; Ohio Myself; Ohio Klan
In *Greenfield Review* (Summer–Autumn 1983): 132. Uncollected.

Oberlin Negroes; Oberlin, Ohio; The Tap House, South Main Street, Oberlin Ohio; Oberlinian Quartet
In *Quilt* 4, Issue 4 (1984). Uncollected.

The Point
In *Pen Pal*, nos. 2/3 (Spring 1977). Uncollected.

Night Letter to John A. Williams
In *The Black Scholar* 12, no. 5 (September/October 1981: Black Literature feature): 24. Uncollected.

Crossing Brooklyn Bridge at 4 O' Clock in the Morning, August 4th, 1979
In *West Hills Review* 2 (Fall 1980): 80; reprinted in *Walt Whitman: The Measure of His Song*, eds. Jim Perlman, Ed Folsom, Dan Campion (Duluth: Holy Cow! Press, 1998): 378. Uncollected.

A Cat By Any Name

In *River Styx*, no. 17 (1985): 56–57. The story of Hernton's and Ishmael Reed's first meeting at the Five Spot in New York is told in stanzas 3 and 4 and also recounted in Baraka, *Autobiography* (181–82), and in Reed, "LeRoi Jones/ Amiri Baraka and Me," in *Transition*, no. 114 (2014).

Grenada, October 1983

In *The Black Scholar* 18, nos. 4/5. Uncollected. Dessima Williams was named Grenada's ambassador to the United States by Prime Minister Maurice Bishop in 1980; the Reagan administration refused to accept her credentials. Bishop was murdered in August 1983, and Williams was arrested the following year by US Immigration and Naturalization Service (INS) operatives while attending a peace conference at Howard University.

Stars Bleed

Black Culture, 1987 (July/Aug–Sept/Oct 1987): 21. Uncollected.

Michael Stewart — Enunciation

In *The Black Scholar* 19, nos. 4/5 (July/Aug–Sept/Oct.1988: "Word Within a Word"): 57. Uncollected. Artist Michael Stewart died in police custody after his arrest for graffitiing at First Avenue Station, New York, sparking protests and a lawsuit by his family. Spike Lee dedicated *Do the Right Thing* (1988) to Stewart's family and other victims of police violence in New York.

NOTES FOR THE RED CRAB GANG AND BLACK RIVER POEMS

The Red Crab Gang and Black River Poems (Ishmael Reed Publishing Co., 1999). "Black River Poem" was first printed in the *Greenfield Review* (Summer–Autumn 1983).

NOTES FOR UNPUBLISHED WORK

Material taken from Rosey Pool Papers, TS 17/19 (verse), Folder H, Calvin Hernton, University of Sussex Special Collections [RPP] and Calvin C. Hernton Collection, MSS14, Ohio University Libraries, Mahn Center for Archives and Special Collections [OUL].

Materials from RPP are included in a folder of poems sent to Rosey Pool, presumably for consideration in the 1962 anthology *Beyond the Blues*. These include "Huntsville, Alabama," one of Hernton's earliest poems, first published in *MM*; "The Long Blues," first published in *Umbra*; "A Being Exit in the World," first published in *Beyond the Blues* and *Sixes and Sevens*; "Blues for Handy," first printed in *Negro Digest*; and the unpublished poems "You

Take a Country Like America," "Poor Mildred's Delicatessen," "The Dream,"
"Poem ('We who love are denied love')," and "Dancing to the Rhythm."
Materials from OUL date from the 1950s to the late 1970s.

You Take a Country Like America

    RSP. Typescript.

Poor Mildred's Delicatessen

    RSP. Typescript.

Calvin Hernton Seeks to Build and Preserve a House

    OUL, Box 2, Folder 1. Typescript, handwritten corrections, signed. Stanza 1:
"True House": handwritten emendation to "Temple." Final line of section 1:
"And die" corrected to "And pray." Section II, stanza 1: originally "Christ died
but he rose, and / Likewise, upon the third day when you return, / I shall
also rise." Section III, final line of penultimate stanza, phrase deleted: "I
hear confused, hopeless tongues uttering / hopeful words in a lost world."
Section IV, final line: "tearful face" was originally "throbbing, dead face."
Section V, opening lines: "Once erected, even then the True House / Is not
so easily preserved" was originally "Once erected, how shall the house / be
preserved?" Section VI: additional stanza following opening three lines was
removed; not included in this volume.

When Soothsayers Black

    OUL, Box 2, Folder 1. Typescript, handwritten corrections. Handwritten
variant title: "When Soothsayers Black."

Deep Sea Blues

    OUL, Box 2, Folder 2. Typescript, handwritten corrections, signed.

Id and Ego

    OUL, Box 2, Folder 2. Typescript, handwritten corrections, signed. First
stanza marked "re-structure."

1961

    OUL, Box 2, Folder 2, Calvin C. Hernton Collection MSS14, Ohio
University. Typescript, signed.

Southern Laughter

    Box 2, Folder 3, Calvin C. Hernton Collection MSS14, Ohio University.
Typescript, handwritten corrections.

Statement

    OUL, Box 2, Folder 3. Typescript, handwritten corrections. Dedication: "for
the class of 1954," with "Talladega College" written at bottom of the page.

Black Metathesis

    OUL, Box 2, Folder 4. Typescript, handwritten corrections, signed "Calvin

C. Hernton, 14 Avenue A, # 6 New York 9." First half of poem (three stanzas) marked "omit" and not included in this volume.

Hank Dixon and the Law

OUL, Box 2, Folder 4. Typescript, handwritten corrections. Original title: "Billy the Kid Revisited." Revisions as follows: Stanza 3: "Willie Jones, a black peon in Alabama found an abandoned / bag of rotten cabbages" was originally "Willie Jones, a black peon in Alabama, comes across a ten dollar / bag of neckbones." Stanza 4: Deleted lines after "What does the name Charles Mack Parker mean to you": "What do Sacco and Vanzetti mean to you / What does the jailing of Bertrand Russell mean to you." Stanza 6: Opening line deleted: "Write my name in your files, hang my face in the post office."

A Lantern for Abigail Moonlight

OUL, Box 2, Folder 5. Typescript, handwritten corrections. "First" is written on the top left of the manuscript, indicating a first draft. A journalist and activist, Nora Hicks, first wife of activist Calvin Hicks, served as Umbra's secretary, organized fundraising events and parties, and kept group records; her apartment was a "cultural center" for the group. Variants are as follows. Stanza 6: "Eschewing the feeble impuissant arms of artifact females" was originally "Eschewing the feeble impuissant arms of mere women." Following line deleted: "For men are driven to witchery, also." Stanza 8: "And the duskman of black, spewing death ink into white eyes, is the Master of all darkness" was originally "and the bearded duskman, who has finally harnessed the black forces / of America's indeterminal guilt." This is a reference, punning on the title of the play *Dutchman* by LeRoi Jones/ Amiri Baraka, about whom Hernton wrote the article "The Witchcraft of LeRoi Jones" for *Peace News*. The ending of the poem contains multiple handwritten corrections, in different inks, to the final lines. An alternative, handwritten ending adds these final lines: "As I Caesar section — / Down / On the infibulated womb of God!"

Litany in Winter's Garden

OUL, Box 2, Folder 5. Typescript, with handwritten corrections: two pages of additional typescript sections with handwritten corrections on differently colored paper. The poem dates from 1960, the year of Richard Wright's death, and judging by other references to T. S. Eliot in other poems of this period. The poem is clearly unfinished. Sections I–VI are typescript on green paper: two additional pages on pink paper present three additional sections, with various handwritten suggestions for incorporation into the preceding poem, marked for inclusion in pen at various points. For the most part, the additional pages seemed to us to represent fragments or alternative directions rather than to fit cohesively with the rest of the poem, and we have excluded them, with the exception of the very final stanza, which we use to conclude the poem. We have thus produced a composite, pared-down "edit" of the poem, which seemed to us to approximate a more polished final draft.

The Passengers

OUL, Box 2, Folder 5. Typescript with handwritten corrections. Inscribed "Calvin C. Hernton, 14 Avenue #6, New York 9, New York." Hernton read this poem on the 1966 LP *Destinations*, but it does not seem to have appeared in print. The version we include here is a composite from a manuscript version — either earlier or later than the recording — with numerous handwritten revisions, and some lines recited on the recording, but not included on the manuscript. Hernton appears to have changed his mind about the dedication to the poem at different stages. The dedication on the manuscript reads "For Ishmael Reed." Given that Hernton mentions the dedication to Allen Ginsberg (and Ginsberg's review of the record) in his essay "Les Deux Megots Mon Amor," we have printed the poem with the Ginsberg dedication. Stanza 6: Lines from "pee-peeing like average men and women" to "pee-peeing in locker rooms taken"; from "getting in and out of taxicabs, solemn, serene" to "throughout the teeming cities"; and from "mixing with communists" to "negro prostitutes" have been taken from the audio recording.

Wooing of the Little Girl Who Lives in a Dark Hall

OUL, Box 2, Folder 5. Typescript, handwritten corrections with additional corrections. Inscribed "Calvin Hernton, May 1962, NYC."

Mad Dogs in Vietnam

OUL, Box 2, Folder 7. Typescript, handwritten corrections. Inscribed "Calvin Hernton, 164 Southgate Road, London, N1, 1966."

A Canticle for the 1960s

OUL, Box 2, Folder 6. Dedication: "For Ree Dragonette, in memorial." Our text is a composite from two typescript versions of the poem with handwritten corrections, the second marked "rough draft, corrected, revised."

Selected Bibliography

BOOKS BY CALVIN C. HERNTON

The Coming of Chronos to the House of Nightsong: An Epical Narrative of the South (New York: Interim Books, 1964).

Sex and Racism in America (Garden City, New York: Doubleday, 1965).

White Papers for White Americans (Garden City, New York: Doubleday, 1966).

Coming Together: Black Power, White Hatred, and Sexual Hang-Ups (New York: Random House, 1971).

The Cannabis Experience: An Interpretative Study of the Effects of Marijuana and Hashish (with Joseph Berke; London: P. Owen, 1974).

Scarecrow (Garden City, New York: Doubleday, 1974).

Medicine Man: Collected Poems (Berkeley, CA: Reed, Cannon & Johnson, 1976).

The Sexual Mountain and Black Women Writers: Adventures in Sex, Literature, and Real Life (New York: Anchor/Doubleday, 1987).

The Red Crab Gang and Black River Poems (Berkeley, CA: Ishmael Reed Publishing Co., 1999).

Power and Transformation: Black Women and White Women in American Democracy — A New Approach. Unpublished manuscript.

UNCOLLECTED WORK BY CALVIN C. HERNTON

Poetry by Calvin C. Hernton

"Little Rock, U.S.A.," in *Black and Unknown Bards: A Collection of Negro Poetry,* eds. Eric Walrond and Rosey Pool (Aldington, Kent: Hand and Flower Press, 1958).

"Thespian," in *Beyond the Blues,* ed. Rosey E. Pool (Lympne, Kent: Hand and Flowers Press, 1962).

"Neto and Meloise," in *The Black Scholar* 19, no. 4/5 (July/Aug–Sept/Oct 1988): 57.

"We are Demon," in *A Gathering of the Tribes,* issue 8 (1998): 27–28.

Fiction by Calvin C. Hernton

"Never Alone in the World," in *Freedomways* (Spring 1963): 184–91.

"Dew's Song" (1990), in *Erotique Noir / Black Erotica*, eds. Miriam DeCosta-Willis, Reginald Martin, Roseann P. Bell (London: Doubleday, 1992): 119–25.

Essays by Calvin C. Hernton

"White Liberals and Black Muslims," in *Negro Digest* 12, no. 12 (October 1963): 3–11.

"Is There *Really* a Negro Revolution?," in *Negro Digest* 14, no. 2 (December 1964): 10–22. Revised and reprinted as "Grammar of the Negro Revolution" in *White Papers for White Americans*.

"On Racial Riots in America," in *Peace News* (March 25, 1966).

"The Witchcraft of LeRoi Jones," in *Peace News* (April 15, 1966).

"Going Back South," in *Dissent* (May 1966): 265–74. Revised as part of "The Debt I Owe" in *White Papers for White Americans*.

"Dynamite Growing Out of Their Skulls!," in *Black Fire: An Anthology of Afro-American Writing*, eds. Amiri Baraka and Larry Neal (New York: Morrow, 1968).

"Racism and the Sexual Under Currents," in *Penthouse* (London) 4, no. 4 (1969).

"Social Struggle and Sexual Conflict," in *Sexuality: A Search for Perspective*, eds. D. L. Grummon and A. M. Barclay (New York: Van Nostrand Reinhold, 1971).

"The Passion of Robert Hayden," in *Obsidian* 8, no. 1 (Spring 1982: "A Robert Hayden Special Issue"): 176–81.

"The Sexual Mountain and Black Women Writers," in *Black American Literature Forum* 18, no. 4 (Winter 1984): 139–145. Reprinted in the book of the same name.

"On Being a Male Anti-Sexist," in *The American Voice*, no. 5 (Winter 1986): 74–101.

Introduction to Janheinz Jahn, *Muntu: African Culture and the Western World* (New York, Grove Weidenfeld, 1990).

Introduction to Chester Himes, *The Collected Stories of Chester Himes* (New York: Thunder's Mouth Press, 1990).

"Shining: Robert Hayden's *Runagate, Runagate*," in *Field* 47 (Autumn 1992): 34–40. Reprinted in *Robert Hayden: Essays on the Poetry*, eds. Laurence

Goldstein and Robert Chrisman (Ann Arbor: University of Michigan Press, 2001): 322–28.

"The Poetic Consciousness of Langston Hughes: From Affirmation to Revolution," in *Langston Hughes Review* (Spring 1993).

"Umbra: A Personal Recounting," in *African American Review* 27, no. 4 (Winter 1993): 579–84.

"Chattanooga Black Boy: Identity and Racism," in *Names We Call Home: Autobiography on Racial Identity*, eds. Becky Thompson and Sangeeta Tyagi (London and New York: Routledge, 1996).

"Between History and Me: Persecution, Paranoia and the Police," in *Even Paranoids Have Enemies: New Perspectives on Paranoia And Persecution*, eds. Joseph Berke, Stella Pierides, Andrea Sabbadini, and Stanley Schneider (London and New York: Routledge, 1998):166–76.

"Les Deux Megots Mon Amour" (1985), in *Light Years: An Anthology on Sociocultural Happenings (Multimedia in the East Village, 1960–1966)*, ed. Carol Bergé (New York: Spuyten Duyvil, 2010): 291–308.

"Breaking Silences," in *Traps: African American Men on Gender and Sexuality*, eds. Rudolph P. Byrd and Beverly Guy-Sheftall (Bloomington: Indiana University Press, 2001): 154–57.

Recordings by Calvin C. Hernton

Contributions to *Black Zero*, installation by Aldo Tambellini, premiered in New York, 1965; revived at the Tate Modern in London, 2012.

On *Destinations: Four Contemporary Poets* (with N. H. Pritchard, Paul Blackburn, and Jerome Badanes; Essence Records LP, 1966).

On *New Jazz Poets*, compiled and edited by Walter Lowenfels (Smithsonian Folkways LP, 1967).

Anthologies with Contributions by Calvin C. Hernton

Walrond, Eric, and Rosey Pool, eds. *Black and Unknown Bards: A Collection of Negro Poetry* (Aldington, Kent: Hand and Flower Press, 1958).

Pool, Rosey E., and Paul Breman, eds. *Ik Zag Hoe Zwart Ik Was / I Saw How Black I Was: Poetry of North American Negroes: A Bilingual Anthology* (Den Haag, Bert Bakker / Daamen NV, 1958).

Pool, Rosey, ed. *Beyond the Blues* (Lympne, Kent, UK: Hand and Flowers Press, 1962).

Breman, Paul, ed. *Sixes and Sevens* (London: Paul Breman, 1962).

Hughes, Langston, ed. *New Negro Poets: U.S.A.* (Bloomington: Indiana University Press, 1964).

Hayden, Robert, ed. *Kaleidoscope: Poems by American Negro Poets* (New York: Harcourt, Brace & World, 1967).

Baraka, Amiri, and Larry Neal, eds. *Black Fire* (New York: William Morrow, 1968).

Adoff, Arnold, ed. *I am the Darker Brother: An Anthology of Modern Poems by African-Americans* (New York: Macmillan, 1968; revised edition, 1997).

Lowenfels, Walter, ed. *In a Time of Revolution: Poems from Our Third World* (New York: Random House, 1969).

Major, Clarence, ed. *The New Black Poetry* (New York: International Publishers, 1969).

Reed, Ishmael, ed. *19 Necromancers from Now* (New York: Doubleday, 1970).

Jordan, June, ed. *Soulscript: A Collections of Classic African-American Poetry* (New York: Doubleday, 1970).

Adoff, Arnold, and Alvin C. Hollingsworth, eds. *Black Out Loud: An Anthology of Modern Poems by Black Americans* (New York: Macmillan, 1970).

Miller, Adam David, ed. *Dices or Black Bones: Black Voices of the Seventies* (Boston: Houghton Mifflin, 1970).

Baylor, Robert, and Brenda Stokes, eds. *Fine Frenzy: Enduring Themes in Poetry* (New York: McGraw-Hill, 1972).

Adoff, Arnold, ed. *The Poetry of Black America: Anthology of the 20th Century* (New York: Harper and Rowe, 1973).

Breman, Paul, ed. *You Better Believe It* (London: Penguin, 1973).

DeCosta-Willis, Miriam, Reginald Martin, and Roseann P. Bell, eds. *Erotique Noir / Black Erotica* (London: Doubleday, 1992).

Hedin, Robert, and Michael Waters, eds. *Perfect in Their Art: Poems on Boxing from Homer to Ali* (Carbondale: Southern Illinois University Press, 2003).

Gates Jr., Henry Louis, and Valerie Smith, eds. *The Norton Anthology of African-American Literature* (New York: W. W. Norton, 3rd edition, 2014).

Young, Kevin, ed. *Jazz Poems* (New York: Knopf, 2006).

Nielsen, Aldon Lynn, and Lauri Ramey (Scheyer), eds. *Every Goodbye Ain't Gone: An Anthology of Innovative Poetry by African-Americans* (Tuscaloosa: University of Alabama Press, 2006).

Ramey (Scheyer), Lauri, ed. *The Heritage Series of Black Poetry, 1962–1975: A Research Compendium* (London: Routledge, 2008).

Harbold, Hilary, and Arnold Rampersad, eds. *The Oxford Anthology of African-American Poetry* (Oxford: Oxford University Press, 2008).

Rowell, Charles H., ed. *Angles of Ascent: A Norton Anthology of Contemporary African American Poetry* (New York: W. W. Norton, 2013).

Young, Kevin, ed. *African American Poetry: 250 Years of Struggle & Song* (New York: A Library of America Anthology, 2020).

Selected Critical Discussion

Raphael, Lennox. "A Remarkable Allegory," review of *The Coming of Chronos*, in *Freedomways* 4, no. 2 (Second Quarter 1964): 279.

Salaam, Kalamu ya. Review of *Coming Together* in *Black World* (November 1971): 93–98.

Perkins, Huel D. Review of *Scarecrow* in *Black World* 24, no. 8 (June 1975): 91–93.

Dent, Tom. "A Voice from a Tumultuous Time," review of *Medicine Man*, in *Obsidian* 6 (Spring–Summer 1980): 103–6.

Magistrale, Anthony S. "Calvin Hernton," in *Dictionary of Literary Biography* 38: *Afro-American Writers after 1955: Dramatists and Prose Writers*. Edited by Thadious M. Davis and Trudier Harris. Detroit: Gale Research Co., 1985.

Tate, Claudia. "Reshuffling the Deck; Or (Re)Reading Race and Gender in Black Women's Writing." Review of *The Sexual Mountain*, and of work by Gloria T. Hull, Susan Willis, and Hazel V. Carby, in *Tulsa Studies in Women's Literature* 7, no. 1 (Spring 1988): 119–132.

Chevalier, Tracy. "Calvin Hernton," in *Contemporary Poets*. Edited by Tracy Chevalier. Chicago: St. James Press, 1991.

Thomas, Lorenzo. *Extraordinary Measures: Afrocentric Modernism and Twentieth Century American Poetry*. Tuscaloosa: University of Alabama Press, 2000.

Nielsen, Aldon Lynn, and Lauri Ramey (Scheyer). Introduction to *Every Goodbye Ain't Gone: An Anthology of Innovative Poetry by African-Americans*. Tuscaloosa: University of Alabama Press, 2006.

Ramey (Scheyer), Lauri. "Calvin C. Hernton: Portrait of a Poet," in *The Heritage Series of Black Poetry, 1962–1975: A Research Compendium*. Edited by Lauri Ramey (Scheyer). London: Routledge, 2008.

Ramey (Scheyer), Lauri. "Calvin C. Hernton," in *Encyclopedia of African American Literature*. Edited by Hans Ostrom and J. David Macey Jr. Westport, CT and London: Greenwood Press, 2005.

Oren, Michel. "The Enigmatic Career of Hernton's *Scarecrow*," in *Callaloo* 29, no. 2 (2006): 608–618.

Ramey (Scheyer), Lauri. "Calvin C. Hernton," in *Encyclopedia of African-American Literature*. Edited by Wilfred D. Samuels. New York: Facts on File, 2008.

Maxwell, William J. *F. B. Eyes: How J. Edgar Hoover's Ghostreaders Framed African-American Literature*. Princeton: Princeton University Press, 2015.

Grundy, David. *A Black Arts Poetry Machine: Amiri Baraka and the Umbra Poets*. London: Bloomsbury, 2019.

Ramey (Scheyer), Lauri. *A History of African American Poetry*. Cambridge: Cambridge University Press, 2019.

Index of Titles

Index of First Lines

Moon and sun, 81
Moon out of orbit, 34
My name is Eleanor Nightsong, 45

No man shall write my epitaph, 6
No stars fell on Alabama, 31
North of Dark, 76
Now floating around Europe . . . , 111

Ohio, I wear you like stepping into
    pants, 126
Oh, love spat upon and made
    mockery of!, 138
Once dawn, 185
One hundred years the world has
    leaked . . . , 65
Out of print, 137
Out somewhere I know a street, 24
Out there in the cold, cruel world, 173

People stop me along the street, 161
Physically, as a cohesive, functioning
    group, Umbra . . . , 13
Prior to beginning was always, 26

Reach! Put 'em up. Put your hands in
    the air, 122
Red, 146
River of the black, 158

Sometimes I wish I, 9
Summer sets on the cities like a hen,
    104

Taste of salt in the skin, 56
The hand who ravished a continent, 4
The Jackal of the flesh howls in hollow
    of the mind, 176
The law!, 174
The only joint inside of city limits, 130
There will be no Holy Savior crying
    out this year, 106
These days when broomriders black,
    169
The spark that will set off dynamite
    . . . , 101
This is the way the poem came to me,
    43

Unreal city, 180

Wall, 8
Where shall the monument begin,
    166
White folks in public park, 171
White sheets, 126

Young Negro poet, 10
Your heads are full of, 173

About the Author

CALVIN COOLIDGE HERNTON was a renowned scholar and prolific author in multiple genres. Cofounder of the Umbra Poets Workshop, participant in R. D. Laing's Kingsley Hall, faculty member at the Antiuniversity of London, and professor at Oberlin College, Hernton counted among his friends bell hooks, Toni Morrison, Ishmael Reed, and Odetta. Celebrated as a teacher, cultural critic, and social commentator, he primarily considered himself to be a poet, an art that he devotedly practiced for the entirety of his life.

Hernton was born on April 28, 1932, in Chattanooga, Tennessee. Majoring in sociology so he could follow in the footsteps of W. E. B. Du Bois, he earned a BA at Talladega College and MA at Fisk University. In 1958, he married Mildred Webster, a Talladega classmate, and had one son, Antone. He decided to commit himself to the life of a professional writer and moved to New York City, where he worked as a social worker and researcher, and was mentored by Langston Hughes. While in New York, his poetry began to appear in historic anthologies such as Rosey Pool's *Beyond the Blues*, Paul Breman's *Sixes and Seven*, and Langston Hughes's *New Negro Poets: U.S.A.*

In the summer of 1962, Hernton was a cofounder, along with Tom Dent and David Henderson, of the Umbra Poets Workshop and its associated magazine, which published the work of writers such as Ishmael Reed, Lorenzo Thomas, and Alice Walker, who became Hernton's friends. In 1965, he published his landmark sociological study *Sex and Racism in America*, which continues to be widely read and taught more than fifty years later. In this prescient and provocative book, Hernton examined the intersections of American history, policies, and social politics with race, class, and gender relations.

As a result of the controversy caused by the bold honesty of *Sex and Racism in America*, Hernton relocated to London where he studied at the Institute of Phenomenological Studies, directed by R. D. Laing at Kingsley Hall. In 1968, Hernton joined the faculty of the Antiuniversity of London, a short-lived radical educational experiment founded by a group that included anti-psychiatrists Laing and David Cooper, feminist scholar Juliet Mitchell, and cultural studies pioneer Stuart Hall.

In 1971, Hernton joined the faculty of Oberlin College, where he remained until his retirement in 1999. Initially appointed as Writer-in-Residence, he subsequently served as professor of Black Studies and Creative Writing, and chair of the Department of African American Studies. At Oberlin, he cemented his lasting legacy as a pioneer in the then-developing field of Black Studies. He also earned acclaim as a staunch defender of women's rights and a gifted critic of women writers, as shown in another of his major books, *The Sexual Mountain and Black Women Writers: Adventures in Sex, Literature, and Real Life* (1987).

His final book, *The Red Crab Gang and Black River Poems*, was published in 1999 by Ishmael Reed Publishing Company. Reed was also the publisher of Hernton's acclaimed poetry collection *Medicine Man* (Reed, Cannon, and Johnson, 1976).

Attended in his final days by son Antone Hernton and second wife Mary O'Callaghan Hernton, Calvin C. Hernton died in his home in Oberlin on September 30, 2001, after a long battle with cancer.

About the Editors

DAVID GRUNDY is a poet and scholar based in London. The author of *A Black Arts Poetry Machine: Amiri Baraka and the Umbra Poets* (Bloomsbury Academic, 2019), he is currently a British Academy Fellow at the University of Warwick, United Kingdom, where he is working on two manuscripts, *Survival Music: Free Jazz Then and Now* and *Never by Itself Alone: Queer Poetry in Boston and San Francisco, 1943–Present* (Oxford University Press, forthcoming), and an edited collection of writings about Umbra.

LAURI SCHEYER is Xiaoxiang Distinguished Professor at Hunan Normal University in China, where she serves as co-editor of *Journal of Foreign Languages and Cultures* and director of the British and American Poetry Research Center. Her books include *Slave Songs and the Birth of African American Poetry* (Palgrave Macmillan, 2012), *The Heritage Series of Black Poetry* (Routledge, 2016), *A History of African American Poetry* (Cambridge University Press, 2021), and *Theatres of War: Contemporary Perspectives* (Bloomsbury, 2021). She is editor of *Between the Night and Its Music: New and Selected Poems* by A. B. Spellman, forthcoming from Wesleyan University Press.